Reclaiming Trust

Reclaiming Trust

A Journey of Transformation

Jennipher McDonald

Copyright © 2013, 2014 Jennipher McDonald

All rights reserved. No part of this book may be used or reproduced by any means, graphic, electronic, or mechanical, including photocopying, recording, taping or by any information storage retrieval system without the written permission of the publisher except in the case of brief quotations embodied in critical articles and reviews.

Balboa Press books may be ordered through booksellers or by contacting:

Balboa Press
A Division of Hay House
1663 Liberty Drive
Bloomington, IN 47403
www.balboapress.com.au
1-(877) 407-4847

ISBN: 978-1-4525-1127-6 (sc)
ISBN: 978-1-4525-1128-3 (e)

Because of the dynamic nature of the Internet, any web addresses or links contained in this book may have changed since publication and may no longer be valid. The views expressed in this work are solely those of the author and do not necessarily reflect the views of the publisher, and the publisher hereby disclaims any responsibility for them.

The information contained in this book is intended to be educational and not for diagnosis or treatment of any health disorder or as a substitute for or replacement consultation with a healthcare professional. In the event that you use any of this information for yourself – which is your constitutional right - The author assumes no responsibility and is in no way liable for any misuse of the material.

Any people depicted in stock imagery provided by Thinkstock are models, and such images are being used for illustrative purposes only.
Certain stock imagery © Thinkstock.

Printed in the United States of America

Balboa Press rev. date: 04/21/2014

Acknowledgments

I wrote a book. Wow! There was a time where the idea of me being a writer seemed so utterly impossible—So much has changed. I would like to express my appreciation and thanks to my students and clients over the years who have shown me how delicate, infinitely courageous and creative the human soul can be. Special thanks to the following friends and colleagues for their feedback and loving encouragement: Greg Godfrey, Dr David Moody, Kathryn Sturtridge, Jane Cullinane, Julia Kurusheva, Lyn Robinson, Lisa Webber, Dorothea McDonald, Ora Lefebvre, Tina van Leuven, Timothy Ferguson, Lyn Robinson, Debs Rahurahu, Elizabeth Thair, Natalia Gomez and Christopher Sneijders, Dr Helen Ferrara, Sonia Czernik and Karen McDonald.

Artwork Cover: Karen McDonald

Author's Note

Reclaiming Trust is a story of Anna's journey from sexual abuse to creativity and trust: Through the use of hypnosis, imagination and other therapies Anna discovers herself. She finds that she is not a victim: she can change her mind and move towards a life of trust, accomplishment, creative expression and joy.

This story is thirteen chapters of Anna transforming her past through family and self-exploration, connecting her thought processes consciously and unconsciously. In all sorts of therapies Anna adventures into her memories and firmly held beliefs to discover that she learned things and made decisions in her childhood that shaped her mind and caused her to create, and re-create again the drama and dysfunction from her childhood into her adult life.

Each chapter is split into two parts. One part lived experience and one part healing where she is deconstructing and discarding decisions about experience, both parts interwoven into the story line. The healing sessions in each chapter include hypnosis, breath work, psychodrama, creative imagination and gestalts, all embedded in a story and balanced with humour.

Contents

1 Fairytale 1
  Anna 2

2 Mother 7
  Visualisation 18

3 Father 21
  Reflective Listening 32

4 Sister 35
  Breathwork 46

5 Brother 63
  Family Constellation 68

6 Husband I 77
  Spiritual Healing 85

7 Husband II 91
  Reclaiming The Child 101

8 Uncle 119
  Psychodrama 127

9	Grandfather	151
	Counselling	154

10	Fairytale	159
	Anna	161
	Gestalt	168

11	Aunt	175
	Dance	182

12	Grandmother	187
	Coaching	193

13	Fairytale	203
	Anna	206

Introduction

Reclaiming Trust is a journey into the unconscious mind to find trust. Reclaiming Trust consists of 13 interwoven stories; each story is a fraction of the whole.

Thirteen is a number central to certain traditions of sacred geometry because it reflects a pattern seen to exist in humans, nature, and the heavens. There are 13 major joints in the human body, 13 gates of the human body of a woman, 13 lunar cycles in the solar year. There are also 13 of each of hearts, spades, clubs and diamonds in a deck of cards. The 13th card of the Tarot is the Death card: it represents not merely death, but rebirth and renewal.

Thirteen is the number of the Goddess. Thirteen is the number of the sacred feminine—the Divine Mother. All of nature is the mother aspect of God; through the Divine Mother you can tune into your innocence, your beauty and your sweetness and find that you are indeed trustworthy.

Trust is . . .

        A form of freedom . . .

                It's dynamic and transformative . . .

                    It's an opening up . . .

                          A flowering of the world . . .

Fairytale

Anna knew that storytelling was as old as time but she wondered who told the very first story... she wondered about the very first time anyone said the words, 'Once upon a time...' She knew that she wasn't the first storyteller, but as far back as she could remember, when she was three or maybe four years old, before she went to sleep at night she'd begin to tell herself and her sister a story. In her best storytelling voice she'd say, 'Once upon a time... there was a star... and this little star looked down on all of the people who lived on earth and she wondered why so many, were so miserable. The star thought that she would have fun if she were there, she would do so many things... she was sure that when she grew up there, she would be a pilot, she'd be a detective and she'd go sky diving; she'd definitely go sky diving...'

ANNA

Anna was sitting in the second row when the hypnotist began the first induction. Forty people had gathered at the Travel Lodge Hotel to do the Hypnotherapy training. Troy, the trainer, was a Scuba Dive instructor in his day job, and in his spare time, a Master Hypnotist and Neurolinguistic Programming practitioner. Troy informed the audience that he'd completed the Trainer's Training Program and he'd been a qualified Hypnotist for four years.

Troy was six-foot-two inches tall, with short dark hair. He had a medium build and his shirt and trousers were fitted and pressed for business. His olive skin was smooth and he'd slicked his hair back with gel. Troy's big brown eyes scanned the room while he told them all a story about how he'd taken a group of ten people scuba diving off the Great Barrier Reef. They had all been swimming around the coral reef admiring the wild assortment of tropical fish, when a large three-metre shark silently sliced through the blue water above them. He had told his students to always remain calm and very still if they were to ever spot a shark . . .

'Quite often people confuse fear with excitement and allow their fear to stop them from having many great experiences in their lives,' Troy said.

Mother

Anna opened her mouth a little. She lay back nervously in the wide, luxurious leather chair and he asked her to open her mouth a little wider. He touched her jaw gently as he stood over her. Her eyes were closed so she couldn't see as he brought his hand up from the tray beside him. He cradled a syringe. Plastic fingers brushed across her face. He parted her lips a little further and pushed the needle into her gum, squirting clear fluid into her pink flesh.

Anna waited a moment for the sting to subside. She pulled herself up to lean over the tiny white porcelain sink. Aqua coloured water sat waiting in a plastic cup. Arching like a bridge, the stainless steel water fountain stretched upwards. Anna watched as it began to dance and wiggle, and then settled still, against the light blue wall. Little beads of sweat sat on her top lip, quivering. The blood left her face as the clear liquid spread beneath her skin, killing sensory cells and draining her, pulling her feelings down the drain, pulling her out to sea.

The rush surged up through her head and Anna fell back faint in the chair. Sitting up again, she swished the liquid around her mouth with large round jaw movements. Her numb lips tried to purse themselves to spit into the sink. Saliva swirled a blue whirlpool around the sink plughole. Anna felt the swirling inside her head and she listened as it gurgled loudly down the drain. The liquid dribbled down her chin and onto her dental bib. A long, thin string of saliva flowed endlessly from her lips. She concentrated, wooing her lips to do as she instructed them, but they disobeyed.

'Are you OK?' she heard the dentist ask through a haze of colour.

'What was in that shot?' she mumbled.

'Lignocaine with two percent adrenaline,' he answered.

'I had enough adrenaline already!' said Anna.

'You must be sensitive to it,' he said. 'Just lay back and let it wear off a little.'

Lying back in the chair she knew that it was her head reeling and not the room. The dentist put his pliers around her molar and she wished that she could be almost anywhere but there.

The dentist pried and pulled. He twisted and yanked. He kneeled on the side of the chair and manoeuvred himself to the front, then to the right side.

'Are you OK?" he asked gingerly, stopping for a moment.

'We'll take a minute and give you a rest.'

'I don't think I'll need my workout tonight!' he joked.

Blood trickled down the back of her throat. She could taste it as she licked her bottom lip and the taste of blood made her remember . . .

Anna first went to the dentist with her mother when she was five years old. That first visit was okay, just a check up, but the dentist stated in his report that she needed five fillings. So, within a matter of a week, Anna was right back in his dental surgery. Dr Mead's surgery was in the Main Street. A narrow, dimly lit staircase led to a small dingy office on the first floor. Worn, checked tiles covered the waiting room floor. Orange plastic chairs lined the walls and all of them were occupied. The room was filled with smoke as nervous adults puffed on cigarettes and waited their turn. The sound of the drill grated on everyone's nerves.

Anna and her mother, Merrin, arrived on time. Merrin walked to the desk to check in and Anna stood, waiting in the doorway next to a small table covered with magazines. She spotted a children's book on top of the magazine pile—a book of paper cutout dolls. The doll was naked on the first page, but a fine selection of cardboard dresses filled the other pages. She put a dress on the doll by folding the cardboard tabs over the shoulders and around the waist. The dress that she chose was white with lilac flowers and stiff, just like her mother's. Anna stood the doll up by holding the cardboard cutout upright. She moved the doll in small intervals forward, pretending it could walk across the room to the reception desk, just like her mother had.

When Anna heard her name called from the reception desk, she walked into the dentist's room and nervously climbed up onto the dentist's chair. Her body looked tiny in the large leather seat. The nurse clipped the white bib around Anna's neck and patted her on the chest. The dentist mumbled something to the nurse and picked up the drill. It looked like a silver snake to Anna. As he moved it towards her face, in his hurry, he slipped and the drill split her lower lip. The taste of blood was alarming. Anna's lip was stinging so much that she automatically started kicking her legs and flailing her arms about.
'This won't take long,' he snapped impatiently, 'Hold her down!'

The nurse held Anna's head. Merrin tried to grab her daughter's arms and Dr Mead leaned over the chair and tried to hold her down by pressing his knee into her stomach. Anna fought to free herself—she hit her mother in the head and bumped the nurse with her pointy elbows. Her right foot kicked out and connected with the dentist's chin and he stopped. Blood and water from the drill splattered all over her school uniform, all over her mother's pressed dress. She moved her tongue over her split lip—it felt deep and raw. Dr Mead stepped back and turned the drill off. He tried to collect himself. Anna's throat felt hoarse. She'd screamed so loudly that the room still echoed around her. She jumped down off the chair and ran out. The waiting room was empty . . .

In the quiet, Anna turned to look back and see where her mother was. Dr Mead was there, his face contorted and red with frustration. His fresh white dental shirt was covered with blood and brown scuffmarks from her school shoes.
'She's obviously a very highly strung child.' The dentist said.

Merrin didn't speak to her daughter on the long walk home.

'Get to your room,' she said, arriving at the house.
Merrin followed her and once in the room she grabbed Anna by the arm and the skin on Anna's wrist was pinched under her grip.
'DON'T. YOU. EVER. EMBARRASS. ME. LIKE. THAT AGAIN.' Merrin punctuated her words as she hit.
'No, no! I hate you! I hate you and I'm going to hate you Foorreeevvver!!'

Anna's arm extended, like elastic, as her weight pulled her down and away from her mother's grip. She dropped down, deeper and deeper, down through the floorboards, down into the earth under the tiny fibro house. The burn on her wrist lessened as she allowed herself to imagine a tunnel into the centre, into a safer place, sliding deeper down into the earth. Down, down she slid into the depths beneath, and then she heard it, the water running in a stream below.

Anna landed gently on the soft sand beside the stream and slowly came to a stop in front of her canoe. Glad to be out of her bedroom she stepped into the canoe and paddled downstream.

She paddled for a while before she met someone she knew . . . a handsome young boy paddled up beside her. Wavy, brown hair fell slightly over his face and his olive skin shone in the twilight. He had a dimple on one side of his smile and a twinkle in his eyes.
'You need to let go of that tooth when you're older,' he said in a knowing tone.
'But you only get two sets!' Anna responded.
'That's your mother talking. You can have as many as you like!' He smiled.

୧୦୧୦୧୦୧୦

The dentist took another rest, but this time he was frowning.

'You might need to go to hospital and get this cut out,' he said, looking at her with a worried expression.

'You're amazing, really, not many patients would handle things this well,' he said softly, and Anna could hear the kindness in his voice.

'I don't feel amazing.'

The smell of spearmint wafted past and she looked around the surgery. It was spotless. The equipment was modern. A small, colour television was suspended from the ceiling.

'Have you ever had a bad experience at the dentist before?' he questioned softly.

'Yes, you could say that.'

'Well, I am sorry to hear that, and I'm sorry that today hasn't gone well.'

The dentist was so caring and genuine that Anna felt herself breathe a sigh of relief.

'Are you ready to have another go at this?' he asked.

'Let's do it,' said Anna feeling more confident.

The pliers gripped the molar and in one tug the tooth came away.

ବ∞ବ∞ବ∞ବ∞

The sound of the doorbell woke Anna up. She felt relieved. Her lip didn't hurt much anymore. She didn't get up to see who was there. Her door was half open and she could hear the neighbour's voice.

'Hi, Merrin, are you home?' Margaret called out.

'Yes.' said Merrin. 'Come in.'

'No, I won't, I just came over to warn you about something.'

'Warn me about what?' asked Merrin.'

'The dentist in town is no good. I took my youngest, Kerry, to him and he told us she needed thirteen fillings!' Margaret said.

'The kids eat too many lollies,' Merrin added.

'Oh no, I couldn't believe thirteen so I went across town and found another dentist,' Margaret said with horror in her voice. 'He said she had great teeth and didn't need any.'

Anna took the paper doll out from the zipped pocket in her school uniform. It was crumpled. She pressed it down onto her olive green chenille bedspread in an attempt to straighten out the dress and then the arms and legs. She sat cross-legged on her narrow single bed and looked down at the crumpled doll. The face and head were torn. The legs and arms were twisted and pointing off in different directions. She yawned and wiped the salt off her face. For the longest moment she pondered the twisted doll in front of her. Finally, she tossed it into the bin.

ᛉ ᛉ ᛉ ᛉ

Anna drove north from Sydney, to Newcastle to visit her parents for the weekend. The sun was setting over the tall gum trees in the distance. She let herself in, threw her bags in the spare room and went into the rumpus room where she thought her parents might be. The room was dark except for the light from the television. Their bodies lay outstretched and horizontal in the matching recliner chairs that they'd purchased at a garage sale in a moment of extravagance. The virtues of 'Domestos' blared through the house 'Get your home, hospital clean . . .' as Anna's father, Harry, on hearing her enter, propped himself up on his elbow and asked, 'Can you get us another beer please luv?'

'Sure. Do you want one Mum?' she called back over her shoulder on her way to the kitchen. Merrin had been so quiet and spread-eagled on her recliner that Anna thought her mother might have been asleep.

Anna smiled to herself as she passed the fake green plant in her parents' hallway. She couldn't see the point of having fake plants in a house—or anywhere for that matter. Squinting, she walked into the stream of smoke wafting up from her fathers' ashtray as she passed one stubby of beer to her mother and the other to her father; then in a smooth motion quickly swept the empty bottles off the floor and took them out to the recycling bin.

'I'll have one more, watch 'Sixty Minutes' with you and then I'm off to bed, I'm not feeling well,' Merrin said in a shaky voice.

Anna didn't like watching television. She'd much rather read a book, but when she returned inside, 'Sixty Minutes' was on with Ray Martin reporting on 'Chelmsford', a private hospital in Sydney's northwest.

'That's where you were luv,' she heard her father say.

'What?' said Merrin with a start, sitting upright in her recliner with the footrest still engaged.

'It's on 'Sixty Minutes' luv, 'Chelmsford', that's where you were!'

Anna sat down at the table and watched the report. The room was quiet, except for the voices in the interview.

'Twenty-seven people died in the hospital,' the reporter stated.

'Dr Harry Maily, a fashionable and highly thought of psychiatrist, who specialized in deep-sleep therapy, ran Chelmsford. Patients suffering from depression would be put into drug induced sleep, sometimes for up to three weeks. While asleep, these patients were given electric shock therapy,' the reporter continued.

'He was a beautiful looking man,' Merrin said in a dreamy voice. 'And butter wouldn't melt in his mouth!'

'What?' said Anna, not believing what she'd heard her mother say.

The doorbell rang and Anna sprinted to answer it. She didn't want to miss any of the show. It was Tess, her older sister, looking dishevelled and cold as she entered the house. She'd been to the beach for a swim. Tess had a large beach bag full of towels and swimmers, and she lugged them past Anna to the laundry room. Anna thought it funny that her sister loved to swim after sunset. She thought she was crazy.

'You've got to come and check this out, quick.'

'What is it?'

'This mental hospital that did electric shock therapy, and Dad reckons Mum went there.'

'It's not clean, unless it's Dettol clean . . .' the television droned in the background as the sisters took a seat at the table behind their parents.

'I'm going to bed.' Merrin said, interrupting the commercial. She popped a pill into her mouth and took a sip of water.

'You can't just go to bed after dropping a bombshell like that,' Anna said incredulously.

'I don't want to talk about it.'

'Was that why our Grandmother minded us? I remember you went away.'

'Don't be ridiculous, you were too little to remember,' Merrin said.

'I remember being in an orphanage,' chirped Tess. 'It came up with my therapist once, but I thought I just imagined it.'

'You were never in an orphanage,' stated Merrin tersely.

'I remember a strange woman giving Tess two plaits. Our hair was really long, but for some reason she always gave me three,' Anna said.

'I remember that too!' shrieked Tess with laughter. 'You must have been four or five.'

'No strangers ever minded you,' Merrin stated as a matter of fact. 'I don't want to talk about it, and I don't have to talk about it,' she said, poking her chin out in defiance and looking more like a five-year old than their fifty-five-year old mother. Turning her back on them she left the room. Anna and Tess sat looking at their father expectantly.

'Come on luv, they have a right to know,' he called out to his wife.

'You say a word, one word and I'll leave you, Harry.' She stood in the doorway with a glass of water in one hand and clenched her nightgown across her chest with the other hand.

'Goodnight,' she said, and moved silently up the stairs towards her bedroom.

'Why won't she talk to us?' Anna yelled out in frustration. She was quiet for a moment and then her face softened.

'I remember her giving me the largest teddy bear. He was big and floppy and brown with a zipper in his back that could be a secret compartment for special things and treasures, but I just put my pyjamas in it.' She stared straight ahead as she surprised herself with the clarity of that memory.

'She went away for a long, long time. I know, because I remember. I chewed his hands and feet off. I chewed at them until they were gone.'

'Bears don't have hands or feet, you chewed the paws off it,' corrected Tess.

'Well I chewed it heaps and I remember someone sewing on new ones, but it wasn't Mum. She was there sometimes, because I remember her beltings.'

'Yeah me too, the welts were red and rose—that much.' Tess gestured with wide fingers.

'You were never belted! Your mother and I had a strict agreement on that.' Harry said with authority from his recliner and both sisters burst out laughing.

'We copped hidings all of the time!'

'She's right,' Tess said, 'We used to compare the damage afterwards.'

'Yeah, who was black and who was blue,' said Anna, laughing on her way to the kitchen to get herself a drink.

'A Royal Commission into Chelmsford Hospital will be instigated to investigate the allegations made about deaths and the brutal treatment of patients admitted to this hospital. What really happened behind these doors?' Ray Martin asked the final question as the show finished.

'I'm sorry girls, for such a cheery evening,' Harry said. 'I'm going to bed and I'll see you tomorrow, maybe we'll have a swim?'

'Good night,' Tess and Anna chorused as he left.

'Time for a spliff!' Tess said excitedly, pulling her bag onto her lap and beginning to roll one, the second Harry closed the door.

'Get it shining bright with Mr Sheen . . .' said the little man on the TV screen. He flew around the house with a swirl of tiny magic stars.

'What's with all these cleaning ads on their TV?'

'It's mum's TV—it reflects her personality!'

'You're an idiot.'

'Electric shocks! That can't be good for the brain cells.'

'Maybe mine aren't that bad after all,' said Tess, as she continued to roll her joint.

'What? Your brain cells?'

'Yeah, a bit of mull is minimal damage compared to electric volts directly into your brain,' said Tess as she lit the joint.

'Why won't she talk about it? She's really pissing me off!' Anna said her voice rising to a shrill.

'Maybe she doesn't remember.' Tess answered.

'I think that she said he was really good looking!' Anna said changing the subject.

'Who?'

'The doctor, Dailey or was it Bailey? The guy who gave her electric shock therapy,' Anna laughed as she blew her smoke across the table.

'What's wrong with our family?' Tess said painfully.

'Mum's got a secret and it's staying a secret.'

'I hate secrets!'

'It's The Secret!' said Anna jumping up excitedly and dancing around the room.

'No shit Sherlock.'

'It's lots of secrets!' said Anna waving her arms eerily around in front of her face.

'You're an idiot.'

༂ ༂ ༂ ༂

Merrin had to be doing something around the house; cleaning the house, cooking, washing. When she wasn't doing something in their house, Merrin would love to look at other houses—Exhibition houses. Exhibition houses were architecturally designed houses that were on show and gave access to the public. They were houses without any people living in them.

On Sunday afternoons Merrin would drive around with Anna and Tess in the car as she found one alcove of exhibition houses after another. Sometimes they'd just go and look at some house that had recently been put up for sale; new houses with no lawn or paving laid yet, but the insides had furniture and light fittings and finishing touches that Anna's house didn't have.

Anna wanted to share something of mother's fascination for houses, but she didn't see the point—Merrin had no way of buying these houses, but she wanted to talk to Anna at length about them—whether this bathroom was better than the house before—comparing the size of kitchen, bench space, floor space, cupboard space, just space in general, that Anna's house didn't have. Watching her mother always wanting, always searching for that *something* that they didn't have at their house, and never satisfying her wanting, left Anna feeling sad, unsettled and empty.

Visualisation

Anna was sitting in a comfortable chair, daydreaming and looking out the window. She knew she would have to talk today, but she didn't feel like talking at all.

'Why don't you begin?' he said softly.

'I see untouched beauty . . . White sand as far as the eye can see, rolling waves caressing the shore, and two beaches merge at the headland. My magnificent house sits securely cut into the cliff face. Steel frames cradle wide, double-glazed windows and support a high-pitched corrugated iron roof. The house has magnificent ocean views; the lounge room window frames the blue ocean as far as the horizon. From my bedroom window, looking north, I can see the main beach all the way to the tiny cluster of local shops, while the view from the southern dining room is the back beach. That's my favourite. The locals think it's dangerous, but I love it, it's my private paradise.' Anna stopped talking for a moment; she took a few deep breaths and then continued.

'The light in my house is natural and warm. My home is completely solar. Downstairs, creamy rendered walls and turquoise, Italian tiled floors hold the heat from the day and give the beach house function and beauty at the same time. The windows open to direct the breeze, or seal to hold in warmth,' Anna said dreamily.

'That sounds great Anna!' her therapist said, 'I can see that you are beginning to trust your instincts with this. So, now ask yourself—*How do you perceive trust?*

'I don't know.'

'Well if you did know? Why don't you begin by adding in other things like . . . Where are all the loving relationships?'

'Who's having this visualisation, you or me?'

'You are, but I thought the idea was for you to see yourself in a relationship.'

'My beautiful dog Bella, enters through her doggy door,' Anna continued with a smile on her face. 'The kitchen and upstairs have wooden floorboards that are shiny and clean. The bench tops are granite and the double sink is clear—my housekeeper has been today. Tropical fruits, mangos, bananas and avocados fill a ceramic bowl that I made at my ceramic class. A blue glass chime twinkles in the sea breeze and splashes blue light over freshly painted, yellow walls. A soft eight piece, teal, leather lounge makes a large u shape in the centre of the room and a brightly coloured, woollen carpet fills the floor space in the middle.' Anna stopped for a moment to soak in her creation.

'You've really thought this through,' the therapist said enthusiastically.

'I'm making it up as I go along.'

'That's what everyone's doing! Once you get that, you've got it made!'

'My life's nothing like that! I made it up because you asked me to.'

'Yes! But what would happen if you did more of that?'

'Pigs might fly.' Anna said, irritated, getting up out of the chair that she'd been relaxing in. She paid the therapist and left the building.

୨୦୨୦୨୦୨୦

Father

The nurses were on their first round for the day as the morning sun filtered through the windows and onto the floor.

'Did you know that your father was addicted to barbiturates?' the young nursing sister enquired as she adjusted the bandage on Harry's hand.

'No.'

Anna had been awake all night drinking bad hospital coffee. It seemed a funny out-of-place question. Firstly, because Anna had never seen anyone looking after her Dad before. And secondly, because compared to the alcohol and cigarettes Harry had partied with over the years, she hadn't taken much notice of how many pills he took.

'He's having withdrawals and we're having trouble treating him,' she added.

'They were prescribed,' Anna blurted out, as if that made a difference. He was unconscious, and she seemed to be defending him.

Anna had not been home for years, but as long as she could remember her father had loved being physical. He loved to dig up and turn the soil in his garden. He was good at creating compost and growing vegetables. He'd work up a sweat and then sit back and savour his work, as if he could see the plants growing. After a bit of hard yakka, he loved a beer, 'I like one before eleven or eleven before one,' he'd say.

He loved the ocean. He had been a lifesaver on Bondi Beach for years. On the family annual holidays, Anna remembered always going out deep in the water, way beyond her depth, just because she was with him. The waves towered over his head and he was six-feet tall. Anna was always pushing past her fear just to be with him. If she went for the next wave with him, she could drown or she could catch it. The rush of having her whole body shooting forward, riding that wave into the beach and keeping up with Harry was worth the risk. Sometimes, she was smashed by those huge walls of water, lost and tumbling in those cold, gritty depths with her lungs bursting for air. Round and around she went until she didn't know which way was up. And then, as if from nowhere, his big hand would reach in and grab her and bring her up for air. Anna could hear his laughter before she burst through the surface.

'There you go,' he'd say tossing her high into the air.

'Toughen up princess!' He'd say, treading water by her side waiting for the next big one.

ஒ ஒ ஒ ஒ

He'd been sick for a while, especially in the last few weeks. Anna had travelled up from Melbourne because her mother had said it was serious. She knew he was sick. He was still in his pyjamas. He was in the kitchen whispering a song under his breath,

'I don't care if it rains or freezes, I am in the hands of Jesus.'

That's a sweet little song, Anna thought with surprise. And then it came. 'Yes, by Jesus Christ I am.' That was more like it. Her father was the least religious person she knew.

He was always telling stories, usually tall ones. Like on holidays, when all of the kids on the beach would gather around and gawk at the massive scar on his right shoulder.

In the fifties, he was one of the first people to survive melanoma. He was twenty-eight years old and he drove a truck for a soap company. The doctors gave him six weeks to live. After a long operation, where they needed one hundred and fifty stitches to sew a skin graft from his leg onto his shoulder to fill the hole, a priest came in to give him his last rites. But he didn't die.

'In the old days, I was a lifesaver and I was swimming out to save this little old lady from drowning,' he said excitedly, looking directly into the kids' eyes.

'When this great white shark came from nowhere and latched onto me right here,' he said, touching the scar on his shoulder.

'I got my two fingers like this,' Harry said, holding up his pointer and middle finger together as a weapon. 'And I poked that big grey bastard right in the eye!'

'Wow!' said a little freckled kid in the front row.

'Did you really?' echoed the rest.

'What happened then?' shouted another.

'He swam away with his tail between his legs, and left me with this battle scar.' He finished rubbing his shoulder proudly, like an old war wound.

When the kids had walked off, Anna was standing by his side, six years old and confused.

'Dad you told me that you fell over and trod on that!' Harry laughed out loud and tussled her hair.

Anna's parents were opposites, Harry was blasphemous and Merrin pious. Once when Anna was about eight years old, she was in the kitchen wiping the dishes. Her mother was nearby cooking and her father was chain smoking at the dinner table, reading the paper. Her father's favourite cup nearly slipped out of her hands and Anna said 'Sugar,' as she grabbed at it to catch it before it hit the floor.

'Don't you dare swear!' her mother threatened.

And laughing from a few metres away her father said, 'If you're gunna say 'shit', you may as well say shit!'

To Anna, Merrin seemed terrified and Harry seemed brave. He loved to tell stories and Anna liked that about him, even though they were mostly untrue. He once told her a story, of a little girl who had a deformed hand. She kneeled down to pray.
'Dear god, please make my hand like the other one.'
With that he would make both of his hands curl into a deformed shape. He thought it was hilarious and he'd roll around on the floor laughing until tears were streaming down his cheeks.

Anna loved his laugh, it always came easily and it kind of started in his belly and wriggled all the way up in his big hairy chest. It made a crackle as it went. It could have been the beginnings of bronchitis, but it just seemed to add to the larrikin in him.

He was an extreme larrikin once a year on 'Cracker night.' It was an event that was supposed to celebrate Queen's Birthday, and Australia's connection to her. Instead, 'Cracker night' had every man in the neighbourhood turning up to play intoxicatingly and irresponsibly with fire and gunpowder and dance into the night around the bonfire.

Children saved up their pocket money for weeks leading up to the big event on May 24th each year so that enough fireworks could be purchased to make the night a complete success. Through the May school holidays, and leading up to the big night, the bonfires began to take shape. Everyone contributed gathering wood for the bonfire in the centre of the chosen backyard.

The women and small children were content to watch the beautiful displays of fireworks at the beginning of the evening—the sparkling shapes with exotic names like Golden Rains and Mount Vesuvius, which were breathtaking to watch. Anna enjoyed writing her name in golden ink on the dark night with her *sparklers; the letters seemed to hang in the air for moments after the sweeping motion of her hand.*

The men were just getting started and with each beer the pranks got more and more ridiculous. Risky behaviour was synonymous with the event, and in the end cracker night became quite dangerous.

Merrin always put the kids to bed after the fireworks and went to bed early herself, but Anna would sneak out and watch the other adults play. As she grew older she became interested in the more dangerous fireworks like bungers, penny bungers and tom thumbs. Pyrotechnically speaking, the hardest thing to do is to safely and reliably light fireworks and avoiding getting burnt with accidental ignitions. Anna had been burnt as a result of her own mismanagement; she knew from a very young age that precise timing was involved: you needed to know the right moment to throw a bunger or a tom thumb without endangering others near you. These rules of engagement changed as the men played, and once she saw Harry throw a couple of bungers tied together onto his brother's lap. Ken jumped so high, so quickly out of the chair he was sitting in, it was as if he had been electrocuted—he seemed to hang in the air mortified.

'You should've seen your face!' Harry yelled at his brother laughing loudly.
'I think I broke my ankle,' Ken moaned, rolling around on the ground and holding his foot.
'Get up you pansy!'
All of the men roared with laughter—and Ken was limping for weeks. Another time Anna saw her Uncle Ken throw a bunger at the neighbour's cat. Every year the mailbox was blown off its post.

Firecrackers are small explosive devices primarily designed to produce a large amount of noise in the form of a big bang. It wasn't a proper cracker night until people had to scatter in all directions avoiding the whizzing balls of sodium, magnesium and phosphorus of an explosion or until someone's hair caught on fire, or someone got burnt, in which case the ambulance or the police, or both, were called.

When Harry did arise from his sleep the morning after, he would light up a smoke and chuckle to himself as he remembered his latest 'Cracker night.' He had beautiful hands. When Anna was little he'd hold her hand and move his thumb over her knuckles. She knew he was thinking when he did that. He'd just sit with her for the longest time. Her whole hand could reach around his first two fingers. That's how they'd walk to the shop or to the park. When they crossed the road he'd hold her hand in his, but she could only hold his hand when he wasn't smoking. He smoked a lot—two packets of Benson & Hedges a day.

೫ ೫ ೫ ೫

Anna and her family brought him into the hospital the night before. He had not recovered from pneumonia and now there was fluid around his heart. Anna said that she would stay overnight at the hospital with him, and her sister Tess offered to stay with her. Their mother Merrin, Anna's husband Shane, and their young daughter went home to get some rest. Hours passed slowly. The nurses had put an intravenous drip in Harry's arm and he seemed to shifting between semi-consciousness and irritation. He was not comfortable and the drip made it awkward for him to move or to turn over. Anna sat on the bed to hold the drip cord away from him, so that he would not get it tangled or pull the needle out.

His movement, seeking comfort, reminded Anna of giving birth to her young daughter a few months earlier. When her body was full with baby and birth began, she had baulked. She was afraid; she felt trapped. She knew that she couldn't go back and not be pregnant, nor could she go forward without getting hurt, so she had tossed and moved around just like her father was doing now.

Anna sat on the edge of the bed. Tess stood silently behind her. Her father half sat up in discomfort. She held the cord up and he almost did a full turn so that he was now, upside down on the bed.

It wasn't a sprightly turn like an acrobat, but a slow drugged semi-conscious roll that moved his big frame to settle with his head and shoulders somehow on her lap. Anna softly leaned back into the centre of the mattress and his body moved too. He was snuggling into her for comfort, like a small child might do.

Her hand involuntarily went up into the air, awkward for a moment. Then Anna relaxed and held him, one arm supporting his back and the other his head. His head was wet with sweat but his smell was foreign to her, lost in the whitewash of disinfectant and sickness. Anna knew that he was going to die, and she knew that death was somehow like birth.

Two hospital staff entered the room. It must have looked funny, this big man trying to curl up on her lap like a little boy.

'You'll have to leave. We'll make him more comfortable,' one of the nurses said.

'He looked pretty comfortable to me,' thought Anna to herself, but she got up and obeyed them anyway.

Anna and her sister left the room and walked down the corridor until they found somewhere to sit. The waiting room was tiny with stiff backed, vinyl chairs and a small coffee machine. Anna pushed the button for sugar, and white fine crystals hit the thin plastic cup, then the milk powder, the fine coffee and hot water. The coffee was horrible. There was nothing to say, so she drank the coffee and tried to swallow the silence.

'That was really beautiful, how that happened in there with Dad. He curled into you for comfort,' Tess said. Anna had never heard her sister speak to her like that before. She looked at her wide-eyed, enjoying the closeness of the moment.

'I'm so jealous of you,' she added quickly, spoiling it. She had often been jealous of Anna, and Anna had never understood it.

ഔ ഔ ഔ ഔ

Harry came to watch Anna play netball once. He was drunk before he arrived with half a carton of beer under one arm, an open can of beer in the other and a lit cigarette hanging from his mouth. He was late, arriving just after half time and quickly becoming loud and obnoxious.

'Oh come on, Ref!' He yelled.

The referee blew her whistle, and came into the centre of the players to toss up the ball.

'What a stupid bitch!' he commented loudly, nudging the little old lady who was sitting next to him knitting, when the other team won the toss.

It was the grand final, Anna's team was winning and she was shooting goals, intercepting the ball, making great passes and trying to ignore the fact that she was really embarrassed by her father's arrival.

Anna was the captain of the team and her team won the game. As she took the trophy the other girls gathered around to congratulate each other and all she could think of was what her father might do next. There was another announcement and the girls screamed in unison as they heard that Anna had been chosen as the best and fairest player.

'The coach is having a celebration for us at his house.' Francis the centre said, hugging Anna with excitement.

'There is going to be pizza and cake!' Cherry, the wing attack added.

'See you tonight.' called Annette, the goal defence.

'See you there.' Anna called back to her friend as she walked towards Harry who was sitting on the bonnet of someone's car smoking another cigarette.

'You're not going.' He snarled in an irritated voice.

'Why?'

'You'll get yourself a big head, that's why!'

ഔ ഔ ഔ ഔ

The head nurse came to see them as the morning sun was beginning to shine in through the hospital windows.

'He's not going to make it, I'm sorry,' she said.

'We'll put him in a private room and your family can sit with him as he passes on.'

Anna rang her mother and family to tell them to come into the hospital as quickly as they could. Her father was unconscious, and he was a strange yellow colour. She had never been near a dying person before. What do you say when someone is dying? The silence between them seemed foreign.

The family gathered around, watching him lying between the plain white sheets, breathing very slowly, and the silence was still there. Merrin was standing by his head, Anna was by his side and the others stood back a little. His breathing seemed to falter. He had always been such a big, boisterous person; he usually knew what to say to break the ice. It seemed so silly, not to talk to him now. Anna leaned over near his face.

'Come back and tell me what happens!' She said, in a voice that held more excitement than appropriate at your father's deathbed. After she said it, it seemed to get a whole lot quieter in the room, until her sister chimed:

'Yeah, he's partied so much, he's worn this body out and he'll come back in another one.'

Merrin looked horrified.

'Girls, don't be ridiculous. Your father will wait in heaven for me.' That did it, now they'd all made fools of themselves. Harry seemed happy, and with that he exhaled and he was gone.

ৎ৵ ৎ৵ ৎ৵ ৎ৵

The funeral was better than Anna had expected. People came from all over Australia and after a few drinks it wasn't long before everyone remembered something outrageous that they'd done with Harry, some memorable experience that he had shared with them and started telling stories of that funny time . . .

Anna remembered when she got her license at sixteen, he would get her to come into town and drive him home from a pub called the 'Robin Hood.' That way he got to have a few more for the road. Once, she was driving him home and she pulled up at a set of lights. The light had just turned orange. She stopped the car and waited for a green light. Usually, she'd speed up a little to get through orange but this time she didn't, because he was in the passenger seat. A biker was behind them and had expected her to drive on.

'You stupid fucking bitch, why'd ya stop?' he yelled.

Anna was feeling nervous with her choice but her father took her side.

'Don't listen to him, you needed to stop,' Harry said, sounding very much like her old driving instructor.

'Fucking stupid bitch!' The biker yelled as the light turned green. He pulled the throttle back and sped off on the inside of their car.

'Chase him! Nobody speaks to my daughter that way,' he said.

Anna put her foot down and sped after the motorbike. She wondered where this was leading. The guy on the bike looked huge and he was angry. Her father had an imposing build too, but it was softened now with a three—piece suit that this office job required. He'd been in the pub drinking for the last few hours and he was pushing fifty. Anna didn't think that this could end well.

The biker raced up the main road, weaving in and out of traffic and Anna kept up with him. When the biker realised that he was being followed, he pulled over. He got off his bike and walked towards the car with a stream of abuse spurting from his mouth. The passenger door of their car opened slowly and Anna saw her father get out. She stayed in the car at first and then she couldn't. She got out, just in time to see the biker ranting and waving his hands in the air above his head.

'You stupid old bastard, I'm gunna bash your fucking head in.'

He pushed his left shoulder forward to shake it out of his thick black leather jacket, following with his right shoulder. The jacket fell to his elbows just for a moment, pinning his arms behind his back. The timing was impeccable; Harry took a swing with his right arm and his fist connected solidly under the biker's chin. The big, angry biker hit the dirt with a silenced mouth and a soft thud. He lay there on the sparse grass: awkward, crumpled and finished.

Anna parked the car and walked over to Harry, dumbstruck. The guy was out cold.

'Sweetheart,' he said with a cheeky grin. 'Never worry about the guys who want to take their jackets off, it's the bastards that button them up that you need to worry about.'

Reflective Listening

Anna: I don't know if I will have enough money to pay you today.

Therapist: Oh, why is that?

Anna: My car broke down on the way and I had to get it towed to the mechanics. It could cost a lot to fix it.

Therapist: It sounds like you have an interesting time with money. Do you want to tell me about money and you . . . money in your life . . . what is that like?

Anna: It's like my hands have holes in them. Perforated holes. I work so hard and I get money but I can't save it and I can't seem to hold on to it.

Therapist: You work so hard for money but you can't hold it in your life. And your hands have perforated holes so that they can't hold money.

Anna: It's like going through life with a bucket with a hole in it. Yeah, an empty bucket.

Therapist: As you think that a bucket with a hole in it—is that a good metaphor for you around money?

Anna: Yes, exactly. I've only just realized that I think that, perforated hands—is a weird thing to say really.

Therapist: What is presupposed in that metaphor?

Anna: Nothing really . . . it's just a phrase I use.

Therapist: The unconscious mind listens to every term you use and takes it literally.

Anna: Well it would seem to make everything that I gather leaks away.

Therapist: What a wonderful realization! Now that you have that information, your unconscious mind could change your life metaphor around money—of a bucket with a hole in it, and make the simplest change to that image to create the experience of having money and holding on to it. What would that change be?

Anna: I could get a new bucket without any holes in it. Yes, that feels so much better. And I could fill it up with milk or honey or just good old money.

Therapist: Good! Now imagine this new image to represent holding on to money and abundance easily in your life. When you trust yourself: *what does trust feel like for you?*

Anna: A full bucket feels wonderful, graceful . . . yes I have grace and I feel comfort and calm around having money.

Therapist: Nice, and notice how that feels for you now as you relax and go within yourself, and the original intention of being calm and graceful around having money. I'm wondering how many different ways you can save money, it may be small amounts at first you know . . . and that's important to simply begin noticing that you have saved some money. Any worries or concerns about money fade away, you can forget about it, just forget about them as so unimportant and insignificant. Your unconscious mind is going deeper and deeper into comfort . . . where you will make changes that will be interesting and surprising to you . . . you know.

Anna: That simple change has made a difference—I can feel it.

Anna sighed and sat back in the chair, making herself more comfortable.

Therapist: How would you know when you have achieved saving?

Anna: I'd have $200 in my bank account.

Therapist: What action can you take now to bring that about?

Anna: I'll put $50 away at the end of this week.

Therapist: Good. And when would you have $200 in the bank?

Anna: In one month.

Therapist: Notice that symbol for you of holding money and saving it now, you know, that bucket filled with cream or honey, or money and see yourself with a bank account with $200 in it. Acknowledge yourself in a good way for this wonderful accomplishment you have achieved and let yourself have those wonderful feelings . . . and your task is to find three different ways that you can . . . bring up calm and comfort, now and more and more over the days and weeks ahead, whenever you think of money.

SISTER

When Anna finished high school she had to get away. She planned a trip through Asia. First she wanted to see Bali, and then explore Indonesia and Malaysia. She wanted to travel by train to Thailand. Finally she planned to fly to India and Nepal. Anna was travelling with her boyfriend Jarrad. They hadn't travelled well together from the start. By the end of the first week, she'd stopped speaking to him. She found him to be rude. Rude to her, rude to the local people, just generally rude. She knew that he wasn't feeling well, but really that was no excuse for his behaviour.

Around the same time, Tess went on her own trip. Eventually, Tess met up with her boyfriend, Aaron. Tess and Aaron had their own problems. Aaron had been travelling on his own for six months. He'd travelled from Nepal through India, Thailand, and Malaysia and finally to Jakarta where he reunited with Tess. Along the way Aaron had become too friendly with the locals. He'd picked up the language and he was visiting opium dens. The two sisters and their boyfriends planned to meet up in Jakarta.

Everyone was tired, hungry, hot and bothered. They met up downstairs looking for somewhere to eat. There was no restaurant in sight from the foyer of the hotel.

'Let's go this way.' Anna encouraged the guys.

'Nah! I'm not hungry.' Jarrad grumbled.

'It's getting dark, we need to find somewhere soon.' Tess pleaded.

'Pah pah pah,' Aaron tapped the drumbeat on his leg, not listening to either of the girls requests.

Aaron continued drumming and Jarrad lit a cigarette.

'Brilliant,' thought Anna to herself, 'It just keeps getting better!'

'Fuck off! You're both useless!' Tess said fuming.

'Whoah! Chill out!' Aaron said.

'Get your own room Jarrad I've had it!' Anna said, turning and walking out of the building.

'Seriously, this isn't working.' Tess said, walking after her sister.

It was late. Hunger made them leave the hotel without their boyfriends and seek a restaurant. Tess and Anna walked down the road in the dark, looking for a place to buy food. The streets were dark. They saw some lights on the other side of the railway line, so they crossed over. Rats scattered across the tracks in front of them. They moved faster through the night, lifting their feet higher off the ground. When a sudden noise came from behind them Anna gasped, holding in a big scream, and grabbed Tess's hand. Disappointment swept over her fright, Tess's hands were little.

'Bones and where's the flesh?' Anna thought.

'Your hand's like a chicken wing!' Tess announced loudly in a squealing, horrified voice. It was perfect timing. Anna was thinking about her sister's hand. They both began to laugh.

Together they found the only restaurant open, a dingy little place about a mile from their hotel. The fluorescent light flickered on the ceiling and Anna wondered if it was that way on purpose, to hide the quality of the food. She was trying to enjoy her dry sandwich but couldn't. Both girls had a small bottle of coke and headed out into the night to find their way back to their hotel.

Tess waived a trishaw down. It was the only one in sight, and the tiny driver pedalled over to where they stood. Anna hopped up into the trishaw feeling guilty that this skinny little man would be riding them home, but she did not want to encounter anymore rats either.

Tess and Anna sat in the front and the driver pedalled from behind them. They moved slowly gaining momentum and Anna hoped that the driver had understood the directions, and that they had correctly remembered the name of their hotel.

Lights suddenly appeared behind them and when Anna looked to her right—a big black car was riding parallel to them. A large round man sat in the driver's seat and he appeared to be laughing as he steered his car over, so as to bump the trishaw. Tess jumped to her feet and to Anna's surprise started hitting the driver behind them.

'Pedal faster, pedal faster!' she said, in a high pitched voice as she hit him on the head.

Anna leaned forward and started to laugh hysterically at her sister. The black car veered closer, this time bumping the trishaw and shunting it over a few feet to the side of the road. Tess was relentless, her face was taut, and her voice got louder as she continued to hit and yell at the little driver.

'He's driving into us. Move it. Pedal faster!' Tess shrieked.

Anna was laughing, she didn't mean to, she just couldn't stop; tears streamed down her face as she looked at the fat Chinese man inside the car and then back to Tess, wildly jumping up and down hitting the driver on the chest.

Anna leaned forward trying to pull herself together and when she looked up—the car was gone and the dark street was perfectly quiet.

The Malaysian humidity was heavy and oppressive. Frayed nerves and companionship friction left the sisters travelling without their boyfriends. The high ceiling fans did little to shift the oppressive weight of the hot damp air. Even though their room had large windows there was not a hint of breeze. Upstairs away from the busy traffic Anna and Tess contemplated the tiny parcel on the table in front of them. It was wrapped in rice paper. Anna held it in the palm of her hand as they sat in a huge, dimly lit room on the first floor of the Hotel. She delicately unwrapped the package with her fingertips. The thick amber paste looked harmless and was sticky to touch. It reminded her of their mother's senna leaf laxative on the lower shelf in the fridge at their parent's house. Opium was cheaper than her mother's laxative. Anna giggled at the thought.

'How do we take this stuff?' Anna asked.

'I don't know how to do it, let's just eat it. You can eat hash and still get out of it!' Tess said nonchalantly. 'You don't have to smoke it.'

'OK, how much do you reckon?'

'You have half and I'll have the rest.'

'Cool,' said Anna, who liked to keep it simple, breaking her half onto the spoon and then placing it into her mouth.

'Man, that's bad,' she said, wincing at the taste and tossing the teaspoon across at Tess.

She ate her half and sat cross-legged on her bed surrounded by postcards and paper bags full of shopping. She swished warm coca-cola around her mouth trying to get rid of the opium taste. She used an elastic band to pull her long, thick brown hair up into a high ponytail and get it off her back. Tess had a sarong loosely tied around her suntanned body and she looked comfortable and pretty despite the temperature. Tess had been writing to her friends back home. In between thoughts and writing, she would pull out an item of shopping and admire it. She held her new royal blue sarong up in front of herself, then a new bikini, just to look at it again.

'I love shopping!' she shouted out loud to no one in particular. Restless, she shifted onto her stomach, pushing the shopping up to the end of her mattress and then went back to writing. Anna glanced over at her, from her bed.

'You're so wasted! Look at your writing, no one will ever be able to decipher that,' she laughed.

'I can read my writing perfectly well!' Tess defended herself defiantly. She jumped up and wobbled over to Anna's bed.

'I've found something—I'll show you,' she said pushing a postcard with a picture of Phuket Beach on the front toward Anna. On the back she had drawn a tiny, tiny scribble.

'There, that's me,'

'What's you?' questioned Anna. 'That tiny bit of scribble?'

'Yep, that tiny, weenie bit of scribble is me. I'm that in-sig-ni-fi-cant,' she said, syncopating each syllable.

'You mean that you think you're that mark on the paper?'

'No, that's wrong,' crossing it out. 'I'm smaller than that—I'm this,' she said, making a smaller mark on the paper.

'Really?'

'Yes. I'm nothing!' said Tess, lying back on Anna's bed quite happy and proud of her new discovery.

'Cool,' said Anna, and they both laughed so much that they blurred the ink mark on the paper with their tears. Finally, Anna picked up the camera and aimed to capture the moment.

'I have to take your photo,' was the last thing that she remembered.

৯৯৯৯

She always remembered the searing heat of summer. She remembered her first year at high school. It was one hundred and two degrees outside. Anna tried to sleep on the floorboards because the bedding stuck to her skin. There was never a breeze. She couldn't breathe. Every morning at six, her mother's shrill voice called to her and her sister to get up. Weary and weathered from the night, Anna dragged herself out of her room. The cool water of the shower did little to wash the night away.

Anna tried hard not to notice the noise in the background, a continual nagging drone.

'Girls, you're going to be late again,' their mother whined.

Anna didn't want to go to school. The girls grabbed their school bags and walked towards the backdoor together. They both yelled out, 'bye' at the same time, cutting their mother off mid sentence. Tess skipped ahead and instead of heading down the laneway to the bus stop, she ducked under the house and scampered across the dirt into the darkness.

Above them was a small, fibro 'Housing Commission' box. The east side was slightly raised—about a metre off the ground. Dust particles filled the air as Anna crawled in closer to her sister. They moved a little deeper and dozens of daddy-long-leg spiders wobbled out of their way. Both girls huddled in the dusty space, trying hard not to sneeze and waited for their mother to leave for work. They could hear her high heeled shoes clicking on the floorboards above their heads as Merrin walked down the narrow hallway and out the front door. The girls listened as the front door clipped shut. The engine of the car started, idled for a moment and then reversed out of the driveway and accelerated down the road.

'Are you sure you want to come?' asked Tess. 'If we get caught, you're dead.'
'Where are you going?'
'To the river.'
'What river?'
'The Hawkesbury River, it's not far, it's near Windsor. Are you coming or not?'

Tess crawled out fast, like a monkey on all fours. She straightened up quickly and leaned back to brush herself down. Dust leapt off her blue uniform and danced in the air around her.

'How are you getting there?' Anna asked in disbelief.

'In Mum and Dad's car, silly,' Tess said. 'They go to work all day—they don't use it. It sits there in the car park doing nothing. We may as well put it to good use.'

'How?'

'I cut myself a key!' she said excitedly, holding the key out to show Anna. Anna felt like she was meeting her sister for the first time.

'Wait for me,' she said, bolting back into the house. She slid her wardrobe door open, clothes piled up head high tumbled out onto the floor. Unravelling the mess she picked out some clothes, swimmers and a towel. Anna felt excited.

They made it to the car park by half-past nine. The sun was hot already. They had to walk around searching for the car, squinting into the sun and holding their hands to their brows for a good ten minutes before they spotted it. The car was an olive green HR Holden, automatic sedan with red upholstery. They found it parked in the second row back from the railway line at the railway station.

Tess used her new key to open the door, but it still felt illegal to Anna as they got into the car and drove away.

'Are you sure you know what you're doing?' Anna asked.

'I've got my license!' Tess said, as she put her foot down and took the speed up to fifty miles an hour. Anna looked out the window. Little box houses flashed by on either side of the road. Every house looked ugly, poor and identical. They drove west on Richmond Road, and it wasn't long before the houses were replaced by green fields, grazing cows and horses. The danger that driving in a township might entail was left behind them.

'Do you want a drive?' Tess asked Anna.

'I'm thirteen!'

'It doesn't matter. Look, there are no cars for miles. Come on, drive for a while. I want to roll a joint,' persuaded Tess.

'Don't you remember I smashed Andy's trail bike into the garage wall last week,' Anna reminded her.

'This is much easier than a bike, you just have to steer really, and push your foot on the pedal.'

'Okay.'

Tess pulled over to the side of the road and stopped. Anna got out and walked around to the driver's side and Tess scooted across the seat. She pulled her Indian embroidered bag onto her lap and started rolling a joint.

'The pedal on your left is the brake,' Tess said in her teacher's voice. 'The one on your right is the accelerator. Look into the rear view mirror, make sure that the coast is clear and put your foot down on the accelerator.'

'I don't know Tess,' Anna said nervously.

'Let's go. All you have to do is steer!'

Anna put her foot on the pedal and the car lunged forward. She found the steering easy enough and they cruised along, heading west, for another half an hour, enjoying the scenery. Her sister was smoking the joint and thick, sweet smoke filled the cabin.

'See how fast you can take it,' Tess dared her.

Anna put her foot down on the pedal hard and felt her arms shaking as she held the steering wheel. The car charged forward. The speedometer needle weighed to the right like she was putting on weight fast.

'Is that why they call one hundred a ton?' she asked her sister.

'Can you make it do one hundred?' Tess teased.

'Sure,' said Anna, getting more confident. At ninety-five miles per hour, even though the chassis started shaking, Anna pushed her foot down harder until the needle touched the one hundred mark. Smiling to herself, Anna eased her foot off a little and took the car back to the speed limit. Up ahead the town was sign posted with big black letters that read, 'WINDSOR Population 5200.'

Windsor had a wide main street with a large median strip in the centre of the road and angle parking. Anna parked the car slowly and as the vehicle came to a halt, she had a feeling of accomplishment above and beyond any spelling or math test she may have had at school. The street was nearly deserted in the middle of the day. The bakery was open and they went in and bought up big.

'Do you believe this pie?' Tess said dreamily, enjoying every bite. They had found a park bench nearby in a large graveyard attached to the church.

Anna was reading gravestones when she came upon Andrew Thompson's.

'Check this out! This guy got deported here for stealing ten pounds,' she shrieked.

'What do you get for stealing a car?'

'Chill out,' said Tess, walking over to Anna with a bag of lamingtons.

'You have to try these, they're scrumptious,' she said licking the coconut off her fingers and reading the long inscription on the gravestone, drafted by Governor Macquarie in the year 1810.

'Ah look happy endings!' Tess spouted. 'After he did his time, he was appointed as a Magistrate. There's hope for us yet!'

The two teenagers headed down to the river for a swim. The river's edge was steep. The soil was clay and sedimentary rock. It was covered with the wild and twisted roots of willow trees. The branches of the trees were covered with cool green leaves.

'Willows are weird trees,' Anna said. 'They look soft, but really they're hard and unbreakable and they give me the creeps.'

'That's so random.' Tess laughed.

Anna remembered grabbing a handful of branches as a small child and swinging like a monkey for hours on the willow tree in her street. She shuddered as she remembered one afternoon Tess coming home late from school. Harry was waiting for her. He was stewing when he broke a branch off the willow tree. He sat in his seat, in the dining room, pulling the leaves from the branch, priming it. Anna sat in her room and worried. She kept looking out the window waiting for Tess.

'Don't come in,' she pleaded with her sister from the window.

'Don't be silly,' Tess said, and came on in.

'Where have you been?' he bellowed like a jealous lover towering over her, his huge frame puffing up with rage and filling the doorway. Before she could answer he swiped at her with the willow branch. Tears rolled down Anna's face as she sat on the floor in her bedroom, listening to the swishing sound. Anna watched him hitting her, through the crack in the doorway.

'Big tough man!' Tess said quietly as she stood tall and looked him right in the eye.

ଔଔଔଔ

'What a great photo that would be!' shouted Tess from the riverbank.

Across the river, a herd of white horses grazed lazily. The white mushrooming clouds began to look menacing as they lined themselves with darker shades of grey.

'Swing out and I'll take your photo,' Tess suggested.

'Why don't you swing out and I'll take your photo?'

'Sure, but you go first, it'll be great. I'll get the horses and the clouds in the background, and leave your shirt on. I love those colours.'

Anna didn't want to get her new shirt wet. She'd bought it with her own money from a local market. Sucked in by her sister's newly found artistic talent, Anna pulled her jeans up over her knees and waded out to the swing rope that lolled in the water. With the thick rope in hand and pulling it tight, she walked away from the tree. Gripping it tightly and holding it close to her body, she stepped higher up the steep incline of the embankment. She ran a few steps to the side and then took a huge leap.

'Smile, that's great,' Tess yelled out to her.

Anna cut a fine figure soaring through the air with her long blonde hair flying in the wind.

'Whack!'

The thud rocked her skinny, athletic body. It shocked Anna to the core.

Flesh split when Anna hit the wood. She let go of the rope and slid down the muddy slope . . . Now her clothes were torn and her leg and hip were bleeding and through the searing pain all she could hear was Tess, shrieking with laughter on the grass ledge above her.

'Arrgh. Help me! Stop laughing! It's not funny!' she screamed.

'I'm sorry, it looked really funny,' apologised Tess, scrambling down the hill to help her.

'I hate willow trees, they're stupid!' raged Anna.

'It wasn't the tree. You needed to let go of the rope.'

'I was too busy 'smiling' for the camera and following all of your directions.'

'Let's get you up to the seats and roll a joint and you'll feel better.'

They sat on the riverbank and smoked a joint together, Anna cried over her favourite pair of jeans and new shirt, now ruined. Her sister got changed into her swimmers and climbed down the embankment to go for a swim. It was nearly time to leave but Anna was hurt and didn't feel like a swim anymore. Tess swam across to the other side with a fearless, strong backstroke. Anna loved swimming but she didn't like these dark muddy waters of the river. Thick sharp reeds covered the bottom of the riverbed and it gave her the creeps.

After her swim, Tess drove all of the way home. The trip was uneventful until they arrived back at the car park to find that another car had taken their original parking space. The girls did a lap of the area and noticed that there were no vacant parking spaces nearby at all.

'What are we going to do?' Anna pleaded to Tess.

Tess didn't seem at all phased by the dilemma.

'We're just going to park it here,' she said triumphantly, pulling the car easily into the parking bay in front of her. 'And they'll never notice!'

'They will notice! It's five rows away from where it was this morning.'

The girls parked the car and left it locked and safe in its new parking space and started the long walk home. Anna was limping.

'Don't you get how 'out of it' our parents are?' Tess stated, in a matter-of-fact fashion, like she had known this information since she was born.

'Our Dad drinks cartons like other people drink stubbies, he has scotch to get over his hangover and he washes it all down with cheap sparkling wine, and Mum's been on Valium most of my life. Do you have any idea how that stuff alters your reality? They're not here!'

'They're not stupid!' countered Anna, still digesting the information that her sister was laying out for her and wondering why she herself hadn't noticed.

'They may as well be,' said Tess, sounding very wise.

BREATHWORK

'Your birth trauma is with you . . . ALWAYS! Your birth experience is your basic survival blueprint. It is the distorted lens through which you perceive everything. It is part of the mind, and part of our awareness already and that is why we never usually notice it . . .' declared Shari with absolute certainty from the front of the room.

'Every time we think that we are threatened, whether we really are or not, we use *that* experience as a guide for our future survival. It lies just beneath the surface of your consciousness but the unconscious mind is compelled to keep repeating the same sequence of physical and psychic stimuli over and over again; we recreate it every day—because we think our lives depend on it . . . until you heal it—and the way to heal it is to get rebirthed by a Rebirther,' Shari said with such passion and excitement that Anna found herself listening with anticipation.

Shari was a tall woman with crazy curly blonde hair. She was a single mother, to her young daughter, and her work as a Counsellor and Rebirther was based mainly in Sydney, but sometimes she had to travel up the East coast of Australia as far as Queensland and out to the surrounding coastal towns to run her Rebirthing and Coaching courses.

Anna sat at the back feeling somewhat sceptical. There were twenty-two of them all together in the room, including the trainers—Shari and Clint.

'This has to be bullshit!' she thought to herself.

'In a moment I'll get you to all come down to the front and do this exercise with the whole group,' Shari said, motioning theatrically with her hands to the space in front of her.

'Everybody will then get down on their hands and knees and huddle up to the person next to them, making a line or a tunnel with your bodies. I want you to align the space between your stomach and the floor with the person on either side of you. All of you together will make a birth canal, and one at a time you are going to wiggle your way through the birth canal and experience your birth again.' Shari looked around the room smiling and everyone was silent.

'The top of the birth canal will be here with me and the other end, or vagina, will be over there near Clint.' Shari continued to give instructions.

All of a sudden, Anna felt quite sick. Her stomach did a flip, as she looked around the room at the other people she wondered what had possessed her to come here. She nervously started looking for the exit door.

'Okay come down now, and snuggle close together. Who wants to go first?' Shari asked.

'I will!' said a short, attractive, gentle looking woman in front of Anna. She shot her hand up first like she was in a classroom at school and then dashed quickly towards Shari and the top end of the human birth canal. Anna liked the look of this woman. She must have been about ten years older than herself but she had a grace about her that attracted Anna, making her decide she would like to be friends with her.

'What is your name?' Shari enquired.

'Michelle.'

'Do you know anything about your birth Michelle?' Shari enquired.

'No, nothing really,' Michelle said holding her stomach. 'But I'm feeling very nervous right now.'

'Feeling nervous means that you are becoming conscious of how you were feeling at the time of your birth!' Shari continued. 'Leonard Orr—the founder of Rebirthing, describes this breathing as a technique that transforms the subconscious impression of birth from a trauma into a gentle and awakening event. Orr discovered that connecting the breath brings the birth experience to the conscious mind and uncovers whatever thoughts were there around the birth event.'

'What good does that do?' Anna surprised herself by asking this out loud.

'Once the negative thoughts around the birth experience are released through the breath, feelings of helplessness are replaced by calm and peacefulness. When you re-experience birth in this way, you find your most negative thought—we call this your personal lie, because it is a thought about yourself that is not true, it is just a thought that you thought at the time of your birth.'

'I don't believe that I can remember my birth,' called a man from behind Anna.

'Many people think that these ideas are outrageous,' Shari went on explaining, 'But this does not alter the fact that they are true. This breathing is not a therapy but more of a spiritual practice, a beautiful gift really and once you experience it—there is no doubt left in your mind.'

'I have so much doubt,' Anna thought to herself and pulled at the woollen carpet that she was sitting on. 'I'm hurting,' she thought as her head began to throb.

'Once you find your personal lie, the idea is then to immerse yourself in positive thoughts, or affirmations to counteract it, and this brings about a balance.'

'I don't understand,' Anna blurted out nervously.

'Let me explain myself further,' Shari added gently. 'For example if you were born a girl and your parents had their heart set on a boy—you might think that by being a girl, you are not good enough. So the affirmation or positive thought to change that would be—I am enough, I have enough, I do enough.'

'So you just say that and magically you feel good enough . . . ' Anna couldn't help but be sceptical.

'The changes are made by the breathing. The affirmations just set a new thought process in motion and changes occur through your new awareness. Repetitive writing also helps and new thoughts blossom into possibilities. It is a complete way to let go of old subconscious beliefs and to integrate safety, trust and pleasure into your body and mind . . .' Shari smiled at Anna and took a deep calming breath.

'I just can't wrap my head around it!' Anna said out loud with her head throbbing even more.

'That's okay—it is really more easily understood as an experience. All you have to do is breathe, with your rebirther sitting next to you and notice what happens.'

Shari kept on teaching as the atmosphere got thick with nervous tension, as everyone seemed to hold onto their breath.

'Sondra Ray—the co-founder of Rebirthing relates birth and the whole womb experience to loving relationships. She says, whatever happened to you in your birth experience will re-create itself in your relationships until you heal it . . . ' Shari breathed a deep sigh and continued, 'Sondra has done as much, if not more, to advance the powerful healing potential of circular connected breathing than any other author and teacher since Rebirthing's inception. She has now placed her practice of Rebirthing under the guidance of the Divine Mother in the form of Liberation Breathing®. This new expression of the Breathing process of Rebirthing introduces prayers to the

Divine Mother into the session, and is nine times more powerful than the original process according to the Divine Mother herself.' Shari stopped talking and looked lovingly at her audience.

'God I must have had a shitty birth,' Anna whispered to Tess who was sitting next to her.

'So a good idea is to write down what the themes in relationships are for you and notice those things that seem to repeat themselves . . . that's a good clue to birth stuff.' Shari went on instructing.

'Oh that's easy, my partners want to kill me!' Anna joked out loud.

'Great realization—so there must have been some near death experiences at your birth and you keep re-creating that so that you can heal it?'

'Why would I do that?'

'It isn't that you are doing it consciously, its unconscious and your deep healing mind wants to heal that for you—once you bring breath and awareness to that old experience, you can then release old patterns, effortlessly and joyfully so that you will not create it anymore—instead you can have really great relationships that heal you and give you freedom.'

'That would be wonderful!' Anna sighed, beginning to feel excited.

'This process is based on the absolute truth that thought is creative—that our thoughts produce effects and that we create our happy/unhappy world with our own positive/negative thoughts.' Shari explained.

'How is the rebirthing breathing different to normal breathing?' A tall blonde guy in the back called out.

'Good question—a lot of people do not know how to breathe. Think about it. When you're angry: most people suck their breath in; when a person is anxious they take small shallow breaths,' Shari added.

'The rebirthing breath is connected: the inhale breath is connected with the exhale breath in a conscious circular rhythm, like a circle. For many, the first breath at birth was taken in panic and fear of death. For many, the unconscious memory of the first breath has thoughts about survival and this prevents the adult from breathing freely. When you breathe in rebirthing, you can allow those negative thoughts to leave your body and breathe in deeply to fully experience the freedom of the breath release which will make you feel calm and relaxed.' Clint butted in.

Anna was feeling really nervous now. She was sitting between a very large, stylish woman on her right and a small pixie looking redhead on her left. She looked at Tess who had moved over to the other side of the room and she kept her eye on the front door, always keeping the exit as an option if she needed it.

'What I want you to do now, is to move your chairs back against the wall to make a bigger space in the centre of the room. When you've done that, I want everyone to get down on the floor here in the centre of the room,' Shari said and motioned to the floor in front of her. 'Make a tunnel with your bodies, side by side, each person on their hands and knees,' Shari got down onto the floor and helped people move to the best positions.
'Like this,' she instructed. 'The beginning of the tunnel is here and the end is where Clint is. Say hello Clint, he's our vagina today.'

The group laughed and Clint waved a royal wave. His goofy smile and baldhead looked quite attractive as he looked directly at Anna and smiled. He naturally focused and smiled at every person, taking the time as he scanned the room. Anna watched him taking time to notice people and she felt a little more confident now, when she thought about the vagina at the end of the tunnel. Maybe she didn't like being in the womb. All she had to do was get through it, but it looked like a very long tunnel from where she sat.

Everyone jostled into the centre of the room and made a tunnel as Shari had instructed.

'Aaarrrrh! No, no I can't do it!' Michelle suddenly screamed. Her pain and fear could be heard in her voice.

'I'm going to die! I'm going to die!' she cried. The tunnel participants broke the line for a moment and Anna sat back on her haunches.

'Okay,' Shari comforted Michelle in an unemotional voice. 'We're all here to support you. The great thing to realise Michelle, is that no matter what happened—you survived it all, because you're here with us now. You survived it!' Shari patted Michelle on the back.

'What we can do Michelle, is promise you that we will break the tunnel and let you out whenever you want.'

'Okay, that sounds good to me.' Michelle agreed, ready to give it another try. The group reformed the human birth canal and she wiggled her way through, giving them all a commentary of her progress.

'I feel so fat, like a stuffed chicken in here.' Michelle grunted to us. 'Ugghh, my face is pushed up against something, oh dear!' she said with a contorted face.

People were laughing with Michelle and it seemed to relax the room a little until eventually, she came to the vagina. Clint placed his hands on the top of her head and Michelle pushed up against his hands with all of her energy bursting through, and lying face up on the floor.

Michelle had already passed under Anna in the birth canal, so Anna stood up and broke away from the others to watch Michelle come through the vagina. When she saw Michelle lying on the floor she was shocked. Her face was as white as a ghost and she wasn't breathing. No one in the room seemed to be breathing.

'Breathe people!' Clint commanded.

For the longest moments Michelle lay motionless. Finally, she moved a little and then she screamed a blood-curdling scream as she clutched at her chest and rolled over gasping for air and sobbing. The whole group breathed a sigh of relief that she was alive.

'I died at birth; the doctors had to give me a shot of adrenalin into my heart to bring me back.' Michelle said holding onto her chest.

'Happy Birthday, Michelle, you are amazing!' Clint said, patting her on the shoulder gently. Michelle lay with her head on a pillow, snuggled in a blanket and she looked happy, content and somehow new, as Clint watched over her.

Shari wasted no time in requesting someone else sit with Michelle while she recovered and then stated loudly.

'Come on people we have a lot of work to do today—Who's next?'

'This is heavy,' Anna thought to herself.

It was pretty intense watching Michelle 'die' at her birth. Anna knew that she hadn't died at her birth, or at least she was pretty sure she hadn't—she felt drawn to say it was her turn. Shy at putting her hand up, she hesitated further until Shari prompted a few times more and then it felt silly not to jump on up.

'I'll go next!' she surprised herself in calling out.

'Good,' Shari said, patting her on the shoulder as if she was congratulating her for winning a prize.

Anna crouched down and lowered onto her stomach as she began to wiggle under the first few people. She quickly started to get agitated and angry. She felt trapped.

'Why won't people let me do what I want to do!' she thought, and then she wondered where the thought came from. She had only just begun.

'I'm hurting and I want to die!' echoed in her mind. 'Now that's just silly,' she thought to herself and laughed out loud.

'I want to get out of here! I want to finish it—I'm trapped and people won't let me.' The thoughts came from nowhere in Anna's past that she remembered, but they kept coming and so did the feelings.

'This is toxic in here and I want to get out!' She was furious and frightened all at the same time. Anna felt angry and alone.

'I feel stitched in, like literally stitched in.'

'Well I haven't heard of that one before.' Shari joked. 'We have had a test tube baby once before and we gave her a healing affirmation—good things come in glass!'

Anna laughed because she thought that was funny but she couldn't wait to get out. She groaned and grunted pushing herself through the birth canal of people. It felt like this birth canal was trying to crush her.

'I've got to get out, I feel trapped,' she cried out.

'Okay notice this feeling, and notice where you re-create it in your life?'

'When relationships get too close—I have to get out I suppose.'

'Good realization! Now push yourself forward, you're doing great.' Shari said loudly.

Anna felt tiny and exhausted. She was overwhelmed with the sadness and the anger, she felt sick and suicidal.

'I can't get out, something's wrong, this shouldn't be happening. I'm trapped!'

'Do you know anything about your birth?' Shari asked sitting as close to her as the other bodies would allow.

Anna could hear the concern in Shari's voice. And her mind was reeling with the questions but all she could come up with was that she was stitched in and that sounded crazy.

'You are doing such a great job, and you survived your birth, so push on and you'll be born in a minute.'

Anna could see that it wasn't far to the end of the tunnel. The vagina was up ahead; she pushed forward and butted her head against Clint's hands. She was exhausted, she felt so little and weak but with a final burst of energy she pushed hard and burst through. Every muscle, nerve and fibre of her being was zinging with the bliss of being free, the rush was superb until the words echoed in her mind and hung like a bad smell in the air around her.

'Oh it's only a girl.'

Anna felt the strong disappointment; she felt disappointment in her body with herself. The sound of the voice was not coming from this room, it came from the room that she had been born in—it was as if someone had actually said those words when she was born.

'I'm only a girl,' she said out loud.

'Girls are fabulous!' said Clint with such sincerity that Anna smiled and she felt the tears well in her eyes.

The feelings of fear in her body were so strong it was surprising. At first, she felt afraid and then suicidal—these feelings were so strange, so completely unpleasant until the end—the actual being born was excellent. Anna felt the rush of excitement of arriving in the world and then she felt disappointment. It wasn't her feeling—it was the feeling of the people in the maternity room. Everyone was disappointed that she was a girl.

Her mind was swimming with thoughts. She lay on the ground surrounded by interesting courageous people, breathing it in—this new beginning.

'I had a brother who died before me and I think I was him. I think I was my brother and I didn't want to be here and I died and then I came back again as a girl.'

'Wow,' said Michelle sitting down beside her and holding her hand.

Anna felt so close and connected to Michelle—she lay on the blankets feeling comfortable and warm and noticed her breathing was now so soft and easy.

'What if your experience in the birth tunnel was connected to mine? What if you acted out my brother before me?' Anna asked Michelle.

'Maybe, I have never had such an intense experience as that.'

'Me neither, it felt spiritual and I'm not religious at all. I steer clear of anything to do with religion but this was different. What if our breath is our connection to spirit—that makes so much sense to me.'

'Actually, our word spirit comes from the Latin 'spiritus,' which means 'breath'. So it's like in noticing our breath we notice our connection to our spirit.' Michelle said, sounding very scholarly.

'It's great that I'm a girl, as spirit must have an equal feminine aspect, it just has to!'

'Girl power!' said Michelle, lifting her fist into the air.

Anna was surprised and happy. Maybe there was something to all of this after all.

ଔଔଔଔ

'Hi mum,' she said into the phone later on that same evening.

'Hello, how are you going?' her mother Merrin answered the phone.

'I wanted to ask you some questions. You are probably going to think that this is weird but do you know if anything unusual happened before my birth?'

'What do you mean?'

'Did you have any operations or anything like that?'

'Oh, I was so sick for all of your pregnancy. Your brother Miles died at birth and in no time at all I fell pregnant with you.'

'I'm so sorry mum. I wished I could have met Miles. What sickness did you have?'

'I was just weak all of the time really, iron deficiency maybe, so they tried this new thing . . . they stitched you in.'

Reclaiming Trust

'What?'

'Yes, I nearly lost you a few times and instead of risking that, they did a stitch in my cervix so that you could not come out!'

'Oh my god, I remembered that!'

'No luv I don't think that you could remember that—you weren't born, they did one operation when I was a few months pregnant. And then I had to get plenty of bed rest. Really that's all I did after that, until you were born.'

☙ ☙ ☙ ☙

The Rebirthing training was a five-day intensive—Tess had invited Anna to come along. 'This was something that we could do together.' Tess said.

The sisters had not been paired to work together until the final day. Many people had already had birth experiences and other memories of their childhood had come up to be cleared. In a forty-minute breathing session a person was able to clear past trauma and toxins from their system easily and effortlessly. Each time Anna had a breathing session it was different, new memories and feelings came to mind and she felt a new clarity and a feeling of wellbeing.

On the final day, Tess was with her friends at morning tea. When the breathing session started she didn't acknowledge Anna—she just lay on the blanket and said nothing.

'What's wrong Tess?'

'Nothing. I am just going to start.'

Anna's job, as the rebirther, was to watch over Tess while she was breathing. Usually, the rebirthee, the one doing the breathing would talk a little about what was going on for them. Tess didn't say a word. Anna did her best, trying to keep her mind on the job of supporting her sister, but Tess just lay there with her eyes closed. Within the first ten minutes, Anna began to feel a pain in her heart that got more and more intense as the moments passed by.

'Tess, what's happening?' Anna asked.

'Ah,' Tess groaned and rolled over onto her side.

'I feel a great ache in my heart. I didn't think your rebirth would affect me this way.' Anna stated clasping her chest.

'Arrgh,' groaned Tess.

'Just breathe and it will pass . . . apparently!' Anna suggested, trying to be helpful and supportive. She had not had this feeling before with any of the other rebirths and she didn't like it one bit.

'I have a pain in my chest and it's hurting me. Would you please tell me what is happening for you? You're supposed to talk to me anyway, you know.' Anna said feeling helpless.

She began to worry when it became so intense that it felt like someone had a knife in her chest and they were twisting it.

'Are you okay?' Anna asked her sister.

'No, I'm not okay.' Tess snapped rudely at her.

'Just tell me what is happening and maybe I can help.' Anna pleaded.

'I don't want to talk about it.'

'Tess, please?'

Tess rolled onto her side and pulled the blanket high over her head. Shari came over and sat beside Anna when she noticed her worried expression.

'Sibling stuff can be intense. We haven't had siblings in the same training before.'

'What's intense is having someone who thinks they know everything . . . just because they're older . . .'

'You guys are a first for us, you have to be patient with each other . . . ' Shari said.

'How can I be patient when she just withholds . . . the truth is that she's emotionally retarded . . . She never owns or is responsible for her behaviour and she withholds information. And then acts like nothing's happening, nothing's wrong . . . ' Anna added.

Tess got up and walked off towards the kitchen.

'This is just typical! I think it might take more than a few sessions to clear the toxins out of this relationship,' Anna said to Shari as she rubbed her heart where she had felt the knife, and took a sip of water from her water bottle.

After the break, in which Tess completely ignored Anna, Shari walked into the centre of the room and called out loudly.

'Come on back to the centre everyone! We're going to play a game, a game with money!' Shari shouted over the talking. 'Money is energy, just energy. Let's see how it flows through your life!' Shari was dancing around the room. Pink Floyd's song *'Money'* blared into the room.

'Money, get away. Get a good job with more pay and you're okay. Money, it's a gas,' echoed through the large workshop space. Shari and Clint danced together and then apart. The wild fluid movement and the lights flickering on and off made Anna feel a little dazed, and she sat back entertained and happy.

Anna felt a new rush of energy as she joined the group dancing in the centre of the room. The more she moved the more alive she felt. There was a heightened sense of fun in the room and the scene reminded her of the opening of some TV game show. Shari began shouting the rules of the game out to everyone over the top of the music.

'Grab that cash with both hands and make a stash. New car, caviar, four-star daydream . . . Think I'll buy me a football team.'

'Go and get some money from your wallets.' She yelled.
'Money get back I'm alright Jack, keep your hands off my stack. Money it's a hit.'

'Only play with what you are prepared to lose.'
'I've only got twenty dollars,' Anna said nervously to Tess.

'I've got fifty but I don't want to lose it,' Tess said, finally breaking her silence with Anna in a worried voice.

'Don't give me that do goody good bullshit. I'm in the hi-fidelity first class travelling set and I think I need a Lear jet.'

'I've got five hundred,' called a tall man on the other side of the room that Anna hadn't met yet.

'Maybe someone will have change,' Anna offered, feeling a little silly.

'I'm going to repeat this—only play with as much as you are willing to lose!' Shari said playfully.

'I don't want to lose anything,' Anna whispered to Tess nervously as they moved to the edges of the circle.

Money it's a crime. Share it fairly but don't take a slice of my pie. Money so they say.

'So you play the game like this—You dance around in the middle of the room, you give with your right hand and you take with your left. When the music stops—notice how much money you have in your hands and then continue dancing when the music starts again.'

'The things I do for you,' Anna said jokingly to her sister. The music started and the participants danced happily in the centre of the room, laughing and talking and giving and taking money from each other.'

'No talking, just dancing,' Shari shouted again.

Notice how the energy of money flows to you and through you.'

The music stopped and Anna looked at her hands, she had nothing!

'Money doesn't flow to me at all!' she said in exasperation.

'Is the root of all evil today. But if you ask for a raise it's no surprise that they're giving none away.'

'How would you know when you trust that . . . just like you . . . money is energy and it flows to you . . . and through you?' Shari asked the group, smiling at Anna.

The music started again and Anna got some and gave some and started feeling a little better about the game and then the music stopped.

'Shit! Not again.

'Me too,' Tess said, noticing that Anna had come up with nothing.

'Notice the thoughts running through your mind—these are the thoughts that you absorbed from your parents—these are the thoughts about money floating around the environment that you grew up in and you can choose to change them if they are not serving you.'

'There's never enough!' said Tess.

'Rich people are bastards, and money is dangerous!' Anna said out loud and shocked herself. 'That's what dad thought.'

The music started and the game progressed longer this time with both Anna and Tess receiving and giving money, giving money and receiving money. The music stopped. Anna looked at Tess, and they both laughed that they had nothing in their hands, but it really wasn't funny.

Brother

Harry, Merrin and their two-year-old daughter, Tess, were staying until the baby came. The months passed slowly when Merrin was pregnant because she felt unwell and couldn't work. She missed the companionship of her friends at the office. This time Harry wanted a boy. Harry and Merrin were boarding with Mara, Harry's mother. Mara had had six kids, four boys and two girls. She lost two of her boys in the war and both of her girls had married young and left home. Now she lived with Harry, his wife Merrin, their little daughter Tess and Mara's youngest son Ken, who was 22 years old. Ken found work sporadically, drank and gambled more than he could afford and kept to himself a lot.

Mara didn't mind them living with her—They gave her someone to cook for and she certainly loved to cook. They were company for her since Ken wasn't one for much conversation, and he hardly ever had an appetite.

The house was a three-bedroom terrace, two stories with the bedrooms upstairs and the living rooms downstairs. It linked together to a long line of terrace houses in the same street in Glebe, in the inner suburbs of Sydney. All of the houses in the street were identical in structure. Each front yard was a tiny six-metre square of cement. Some people added a pot plant or two; others grew a hedge, or added a table and chairs. Mara's front yard was bare.

Harry usually drove a truck for a living but he'd been very sick and nearly died from melanoma—he survived. It would have been considered a miracle had he believed in God—but he didn't.

'Big bad Harry, hit me anywhere here,' he said puffing his chest out and drawing a wide circle around his chest with his fingers, 'and you'll hit heart!' he'd say to anyone who was near when he'd had a few beers.

It was a Friday night; Harry had just arrived home from work. Dressed in the only suit he owned, he looked smart but weary.

'These office jobs take it out of you more than the stuff I'm used to—how was your day?'

'We've had a good day. Have a beer, dinner won't be long now.' Merrin greeted Harry.

'Thanks sweetheart.'

'How did you go?'

'It just takes a bit of getting used to!'

Merrin was pale and drawn and heavily pregnant. Her energy was low and she felt constantly ill. It wasn't long to go now—only a few weeks. Merrin tried to keep her mind focussed on making the dinner—peeling potatoes while seated: soon she could go up to bed and rest.

Harry grabbed a beer from the fridge and sat on the floor in the doorway with his feet resting on the lower step. As he looked out onto the paved square that served as the back yard he cradled a large bottle of beer in his left hand and lit a Benson and Hedges cigarette with his right.

'Hello beautiful girl,' he crooned to his little daughter.

Tess, their baby daughter sat quietly in a rickety old high chair at the end of the table and Mara stirred stew and dumplings in a saucepan by the hot wooden stove. The conversation was awkward when they were gathered together in the house.

Tess yawned; she was so tired that her eyes were nearly closing as her blonde hair fell softly across her face. Her head nodded down towards the table top in front of her.

'Who's taking the little one up?' Harry said. 'She's going to go face first into that meal in a minute.'

'I'm not taking her up, I'm knocked off.' Harry said, making it clear to the women that he thought it was their responsibility.

'I'll take her,' Mara said, gently picking Tess up and holding her softly to her breast as she carried her upstairs to her cot. Harry and Merrin talked about their finances while she was gone.

'Ken will give me the money that I loaned him tomorrow,' said Merrin.

'When did you loan him money?' Harry questioned, agitated. 'I already loaned him fifty dollars last week,' he continued.

Mara overheard their conversation coming down the stairs.

'I loaned him money today.' Mara told him as she seated herself back at the kitchen table.

Harry shook his head from side to side as if he was dodging punches. He was angry and frustrated at his brother's behaviour and he was so sick and tired of carrying him.

Harry undid the buttons on his shirt while swearing under his breath, and he placed the finished brown bottle on the polished wooden tabletop and headed for the narrow staircase for his shower kit.

'I'll kill him if he's gambled that money away!' he yelled back over his shoulder as he bolted up the stairs.

He left the room and returned with a towel draped over his shoulder and his shaving kit in his hand. The shower and the toilet were outside, next to the laundry room. The gas water heater had a temperamental lighting apparatus that was faulty. It didn't start first go and when it finally did light, it went off with a small explosion that unnerved Harry every time. He showered and dressed and tried to cool off before entering the kitchen again and heading straight to the small fridge in the corner where he knew he'd find another bottle of beer. The cool brown amber seemed to soothe his hurt and anger over the problems with his younger brother.

Ken must have come in while Harry was in the shower. The women didn't tell him straight away, but when they did they were not surprised that Harry bounced out of his seat and bolted straight for the stairway to get Ken and confront him.

He wasn't in his room when he got upstairs. Harry had to look around.
'What are you doing?' Ken looked up from the side of the cot where he had been focusing intently before Harry entered the room.
'Oh yeah, she was crying so I was patting her back to sleep.'

Harry's body was tight, both fists were clenched and without thinking he raised his fist and struck Ken on the side of his face. Harry looked over his shoulder to check if Tess was awake, and the distraction caused him to take a punch in the eye from Ken in retaliation. Hurting, he got Ken in a headlock and pulled him away from the baby and down the stairs. The force of both bodies lunging forward together sent them toppling down the steep stairway. Merrin had heard the noise and was on her way up the stairs. The brawling men hit Merrin heavily, knocking her pregnant body over and squashing her beneath them as they rolled over her.
'Stop it! Stop! Look what you've done Harry! You've hurt your girl and the baby, Stop.'

They didn't stop fighting. They punched and kicked each other over and over again, no matter how loud Mara shouted they kept on with their vicious brawl, rolling on into the living room, smashing glasses and plates off the table, knocking over the crystal cabinet as they stormed along the hallway into the lounge room.

'Stop it, Stop it you mongrels!' Mara shouted as she took a belt to both of them.

Mara raced to the telephone and called an ambulance. Merrin was lying in a crumpled heap at the foot of the stairs. She wasn't making any sound.

The hospital room was dimly lit: Merrin lay in the hospital bed feeling lost and frightened, she couldn't stop crying. In her arms lay her little son. He was so tiny, so fragile, so perfect and so blue. She called him Miles. Merrin stroked his little face, she knew that he had stopped breathing but she couldn't quite comprehend that he was dead. 'The doctors said he died of toxic blood. You have to get some rest now!' the nurse said.

She touched his tiny fingers as he lay there lifeless in her arms and then the nurse came and bundled his little body away from her.

'I want to see my baby!' Merrin said softly, tears rolling down her cheeks. The nurses came and moved Merrin to the veranda so she wouldn't upset the other mothers.

Family Constellation

Anna arrived at the Family Constellation workshop in her old Torana. Her car was a bit of an embarrassment to her. The paint was dull and the seats were saggy. She had to sit bolt upright as she drove so that she could see over the dashboard. The knob on the end of her column shift stick had cracked from old age and had fallen off a few years back and now it hurt her hand to change the gears. In fact, she had a callous on the end of her right thumb.

She was feeling nervous but happy as she parked her car close to the venue, the local Girl Guide Hall—the weatherboard building looked a little worse for wear with paint peeling off.

Anna thought about the word constellation: in everyday usage it meant 'a group of celestial bodies, usually stars, which appear to form a pattern in the sky.' So as Anna understood it, a family constellation represented the group of people; which form a family, and so are, in a sense *'the constellation'* that a person belongs to.

A smile crossed her face as she thought of how passionate her friend Phil had been at the pub the night before. They had played pool for hours and he had not stopped talking, nor had he won a game.

'Most personal difficulties and problems in relationships are a result of confusion in the family's system,' he said, sounding like a university professor.

'My family was definitely confused,' joked Anna, breaking the balls and sinking two solid coloured balls.

'According to Bert Hellinger's Systemic therapy, the solution to family life occurs when each of its members takes their appropriate place!' Phil added with excitement.

'What do you mean?'

'There is an order to things; he calls them 'Orders of Love.''

'My family doesn't know what love is!' said Anna.

'There is confusion in many families. It is a lack of awareness, and without wanting to they unconsciously incorporate in their life the destiny of another person.'

'How is that possible?'

'Not a random person—a person from their own family; it could be someone in the family that lived in the distant past.'

'And how is that possible?' Anna asked, still confused.

'I don't know exactly—you really have to experience your own constellation to believe it. It's miraculous—you don't tell the group anything when you get up to have your turn, except what you want to work with. For example a person might like to work with their depression or loneliness and then their constellation unfolds—the story unravels somehow. And somehow when a family member was excluded, forgotten or not recognised at their belonging place, someone else in the family takes up their destiny—and then the confusion begins.'

'That's heavy'

'And at the same time so very cool! If someone feels left out of the family system it is because some other member of the family got left out along the ancestral line—sometimes before they were born.'

'Again, how is that possible?'

'Somehow we try to live that destiny for them and that creates confusion.'

'When families have more confusion than love, what hope have we got?' Anna added, feeling sad.

'A lot of people don't even know that they are confused!' Phil said excitedly, jumping off the bar stool to have his shot on the pool table with his hand in the air signalling his bright idea and a broad grin across his face.

'Most people just go about their lives like robots . . . and they never even think about these things, but they are so important aren't they?' Anna said.

'Exactly! So what you don't know about yourself can really hurt you!'

He finished sinking the white ball and walked back to his stool.

'I felt so much more at peace with myself when I realised that my family wasn't loving towards me, not in constellation, just in general,' Anna declared.

'Really?'

'Yeah, really relieved!—Finally I could stop trying to work out why I always felt like shit around them. I actually looked it up in the Collins Dictionary.'

'What?'

'Love—The meaning of love!—Apparently it's an intense emotion of affection, warmth and fondness. It is regard towards a person or thing. Once I knew that, from that time onwards, whenever my family spoke to me or interacted with me I would ask myself: Does this feel like the definition of love?—When I answered no it doesn't—it gave me the reason to move away from them.'

'Heavy!' Phil said finishing his beer.

'What's heavy is that no one seems to notice—it's like the world has been hypnotised to think that *all* families are loving and a hell of a lot of them aren't!'

'Ha that's funny!' said Phil. 'But so very true,' he added. 'Sorry about your family, you're a great person and you deserve a great loving family.' Phil leaned over and gave Anna a big consoling cuddle.

'No really it was wonderful—for the first time in my life I felt free.'

'Hellinger says that, firstly, everyone has an equal right to belong to their family system.'

'I like the sound of this guy—you should tell him to have a talk to my family.'

'And secondly, there is a hierarchy in terms of birth order—those born first, come first. Parents give and children receive. The male takes up first position in the family.'

'Hold on! That's not right.'

'But he works in the service of the female.'

'That sounds better—but you lost me on the first one. I don't feel that I had equal right to belong in the family system.'

'Well there must be something in the way—you need to do a constellation!'

'What?'

'You have to come along tomorrow. Come and have a constellation and I promise you that you will love it—and better still you will find out why you feel that way.'

'Okay, I'll come!'

Anna woke up early the next morning, excited by her conversation with Phil and excited by her decision to go to Family Constellations, but sitting in the parking lot outside the building she was too nervous to go in. She opened the front door allowing the sun to warm her legs. She was taking a few deep breaths contemplating not going inside when Phil poked his head out of the building and walked over to her.

'I don't know about this,' Anna said with a little tremor in her voice.

'You're going to have the best time. I'm so excited that you are here!' Phil said, grabbing her in a beautiful reassuring embrace.

'What you said last night makes sense to me. It makes sense that there is an energy flow in families. It makes sense to me that families get stuck, stuck in hurt and pain and old energy.'

'I can't wait until you see it. Sometimes in constellation I've seen the energy get so stuck that they have to call on the ancestor of a mother, the mother's mother, and even the mother's, mother's mother. Sometimes in constellations, the facilitator had to go back five generations just to get a little shimmer of what love might look like.' Phil said, with sheer amazement in his voice.

'I have to say I am interested in finding out the true story of my family's energy.' Anna said.

'Trust me! You are going to love this.'

'What do I have to do?' Anna questioned him nervously.

'You could just watch, or you could be a participant in someone else's constellation or you could do your own constellation and have others be representatives for you.'

'What's the difference?'

'With participation in someone's constellation, if they choose you, you 'play' the roles of others; maybe you might be asked to be their mother or father and either way the family constellation becomes a deep experience. Many people say that by representing others in constellation they see similarities in their own lives and they are surprised at how intense the experience can be. Irrespective of a person's age, each of us is a child in a family, and what a child wants more than anything else is to find harmony within the family.' He took a long swig of water from his water bottle and watched her face closely to see how she was taking the information so far.

'If you do your own constellation you choose people from the group to 'represent' your family members—it's not acting as such, its following the energy in whatever way occurs to you at the time when you stand in that place, with that intention.'

Phil was leading Anna into the entrance as he spoke. The rest of the group gathered together in the hall. Some were sipping coffee or tea, others were chatting in groups scattered throughout the hall.

The facilitator was tall, with cropped grey hair. He had a gentle face and soft brown eyes. He smiled at Anna as she entered the building. Anna knew that his name was Lucas because Phil had talked so much about him at the pub the night before.

'Welcome,' Lucas said, loud enough for everyone to hear as he walked into the centre of the hall. He spread his hands wide at shoulder height, with a broad welcoming gesture and continued. 'A Family Constellation is created when members of the group represent the members of a family. It starts with one person, chosen to represent the client who is having a constellation. That representative stands in the centre of the group and begins to feel the emotions of the stuck energy, the fears and desires of the person concerned . . . they feel whatever comes to them . . . it is not acting or acting out anything—it is following the energy that is there, in that particular family system.'

Anna decided that she wanted to do a constellation on 'Success.' When the process began, the seat for the client was empty. She surprised herself by standing and moving over to that seat. Once in the 'hot seat,' she began to feel quite emotional.

Anna liked the look of Lucas. She had the feeling that she might like to get to know him better in different circumstances, but as she sat next to him now, she felt extremely nervous and wondered what had possessed her to jump up first.

'Do you want to do a constellation today?' Lucas asked looking directly at her.

'Well I thought I did, but I feel a little overwhelmed now that I'm here' she said, barely managing to hold back tears.

'It will be fine,' he said giving her a warm smile. 'Tears and nerves are an indication that you have started doing your constellation already.'

'I've always struggled with money and finances—I only ever manage to just get by. I struggle to save even the smallest sums of money and when I do save, some accident or misfortune will happen, and it usually wipes out my savings.' Anna laughed awkwardly, feeling embarrassed and stupid.

'Don't get me wrong, I mean I have a lot of things to be grateful for—I've never gone hungry—it's just that life seems to be a precarious balancing act—I always have a thought in the back of my mind, like hanging over me, that something really bad is going to happen, yeah—it's like, life is dangerous and something bad is just around the corner.'

'Good work,' said Lucas, in a soft voice as he stood up and walked to the middle of the room. 'Move the chairs back, and make some room.' he said to the other people in the room.

From where he stood, he turned to face Anna 'Choose someone to represent you!'

Anna looked around the room and she counted twelve people. She looked a little closer—to her right was an older woman in her early sixties with red hair and bright blue eyes who wore a pretty floral dress. Her name was Gail. Sitting next to her was a very large man with olive skin and friendly green eyes, called Randy. Next to Randy was a younger woman with mousy brown hair and a diamond stud in her nose, named Julia, and next to Julia was a German girl with an athletic body and a beautiful purple dress. Her name was Lily and Anna wanted Lily to represent her because she liked the look of her the most.

'Will you represent me in this Constellation please Lily?' Anna requested soberly.

'I'd love to!' said Lily, stepping forward into the centre of the room. Now it was a relief to Anna that she didn't have to do anything except watch, and not much was happening at first.

Lily walked into the centre of the room and stood quietly for a few moments looking forward and then her eyes lowered to look down at the floor.

'What's happening here?' Lucas asked Lily as he stood beside her.

'I cannot take my eyes off the floor, there is something drawing me to look down at the floor.'

Lucas got another participant, Randy, to come over and lie on the floor in front of Lily, and he went over to Anna and sat beside her.

'Were there any miscarriages or early deaths in your family before you?'

'Yes, my mother lost a boy, her second child. He was my big brother and he died at birth so I never got to meet him.'

'What was his name?'

'His name was Miles.'

Lily started crying as she looked down, she talked to Randy lying on the floor as if he were Miles, her big brother.

'I'm sorry that you died and I'm sorry that I didn't get to meet you.'

Anna knew that ordinarily she would be rolling around on the floor laughing at this ridiculous scene but she couldn't take her eyes off Lily and Randy, and the feelings that she was sensing in her body were intense and surprising.

'I'm sorry I didn't get to meet and play with you.' Lily said.

From the floor speaking for Miles, Randy responded.

'I was not as strong as you and I had to leave—the family energy got stuck on my death and the focus stayed on me and I am sorry for that—I think that you are wonderful and you deserve to be successful. You would honour me, little sister, when you live your life to the full. I will be with you, watching over you. I wish for you every success and happiness.'

Anna sat back and watched the constellation play out in front of her eyes. She felt her big brother present with her and she cried for the loss of him. It felt as if all of her ancestors were in the room witnessing her brother, Miles, being acknowledged for his place in her family.

'Come up and join Lily now and share in this knowledge,' Lucas said to Anna. *'How can you take your place in your family, and trust the learning?'* he asked her gently.

Looking into her brother's representatives eyes Anna felt the wisdom and the learning of their relationship flow into her and she knew that Miles was her big brother. Even though she'd never met him, because he died before she was born, she knew that he had been waiting all of this time to tell her today how much he loved her and to say to her—'Now you are free.'

Husband I

Blue skies and white sand stretched uninterrupted as far as Anna could see. She walked along the water's edge watching the hundreds of tiny shells rolling over each other. Air bubbles burst onto the wet sandy surface, as the waves receded back into the ocean. Sparkling water swirled over and around her feet and legs. Anna brushed her hair back off her face with wet, salty hands, and tied it in a ponytail. She watched Jess, her two-year-old daughter, happily making sandcastles with a bucket and spade, and she felt a soft graceful feather settle in her heart.

A huge blue swell of water curved to form a circle, then smashed, sizzling, effervescent around her feet. Repeating waves came in sets of six, one after the other and then a lull. Only surfers went out when the waves were this big. Anna loved to body surf but today she was happy to sit out on the beach with Jess.

'Yiiihaaaaah,' yelled Joe, from within a turning wall of water. Anna looked up to see him skimming his hand along the inside of the wave, standing upright on his board. Then turning the tip of his surfboard up to the sky he flipped over the edge of the wave, and fell backwards to dismount his board. Joe pulled himself forward onto the board again and began paddling out for another one, his body shining wet in the sunlight and his black curly hair stretching down his back. Clouds shifted in the sky, adding to the landscape.

A shower lasted only minutes, and then a rainbow arched above him. Shooting grey streaks appeared beneath the surface. Dolphins cut a curve in the blue, alongside Joe's surfboard. The air was exhilarating. Anna wrapped her arms around her body and hugged herself. She loved this new place. They'd come to Perth for a holiday and loved it so much that they decided to stay. Perth was so different to anywhere she'd lived before. No traffic, no commuting, clean beaches, great surf, a few hours drive north or south. Anna liked the laid back pace, and she especially loved the beaches and the sunsets.

ఈఈఈఈ

They'd lived together for nearly three years now. Anna hadn't married him because the thought of marriage scared her—the thought of marriage had always scared her as long as she could remember—it wasn't Joe's fault—it was watching her parent's relationship, watching her mother's life, and she didn't want to get trapped like that. She didn't like the term 'boyfriend.' Defining their relationship made her nervous, so she tried to avoid it. Mostly Joe was her friend: a companion, and then they'd had a child together. Before Jess came along, they were great friends but somehow her arrival changed everything. It wasn't her fault or Jess's—sometimes, Joe regressed to a little boy. Sometimes Joe was just a stupid bastard. When he drank too much he was an angry bastard. Anna desperately wanted to keep life simple but Joe drank more and more often, and their life together wasn't working so well anymore.

Joe had friends up the coast. He wanted to go to a party in Dongara, so he invited Anna to take him for a drive in her Toyota Hiace van.

'Let's have a 'family' holiday,' he joked, making inverted commas in the air.

Anna dreamed of lying on the beach reading a book. She wanted to relax, catch some waves and get some colour on her white skin. So she took him up on his invitation and drove her new bus north, with him and their little daughter. The Brand Highway was bare—not another car in sight. Anna drove with the window wound down and the summer breeze on her face. It was five hours of driving and Anna loved it because she could cruise, listen to music, and take in the countryside.

They arrived in Dongara mid-afternoon and parked in front of the pub. Joe went inside, met friends and talked for a while. When he came out to the van, Anna was sitting with Jess, who was sleeping.

'Let's have a game of pool and a drink before we head out to the house,' he offered excitedly.

'Jess's asleep. I'll wait out here and read my book. When she wakes, we'll get some lunch.'

The first drinks didn't bother her but the one game of pool turned into ten. The drinks were beginning to show. Anna took Jess down to the beach for a swim and a walk. Hours passed. Agitated, Anna went into the pub with her daughter on her hip.

'She's bored Joe, we have to go and get settled for the night.' Exasperated with his expression she added, 'this is ridiculous! How long are you going to stay here? It's supposed to be *our* holiday!'

'*Shut up!* You're never happy. I come on holidays with you and all you do is nag.'

He yelled at her as he walked off towards the toilets.

Joe finally stumbled out to the van and pushed a crumpled piece of paper at her.

'This is the address, we can stay the night.' He climbed into the back of the van and fell asleep. Anna tried to find the house driving in the dark. She drove up one dirt track after another until she felt hopelessly lost. Finally she pulled the van to a stop. Golden stars pierced the black sky but Anna couldn't catch her breath. Sighing deeply, she tipped the passenger seat forward and climbed over into the back of the van. She would sleep now and find the house tomorrow, she thought. She leaned over to check on Jess and Joe stirred. He woke up instantly, loud and obnoxious.

'Why have we stopped? Are we there yet?'

'No we're not there yet! The directions you gave me were wrong. We're lost and this is where we're staying until the morning.' Anna spoke softly so as not to wake up Jess.

'Fuck that, we'll miss the party!' he screeched.

'You're too wasted; you've been drinking all afternoon.' Anna protested.

'No—we're going to the party . . . DRIVE!' he yelled, putting his fist up into her face. Anna was frightened when she looked into his eyes. She didn't recognise him. All she could see was a wild angry animal.

'DRIVE!'

Jess woke up frightened and started crying.

'Shut up,' he yelled at her. 'Do you want to see me smash Mummy in the face?' He gurgled through the angry acid in his ugly mouth.

'Drive,' he ordered.

Anna got back into the driver's seat. Jess pulled herself back into the blankets, into the dark, whimpering softly, trying to hold her eyes wide open.

Anna felt light headed. She rubbed her eyes and tried to focus on the road, driving back the way she'd come. The dirt road ended and she turned into the main street hoping to stop outside the police station, but as she slowed down, her headlights revealed a completely dark street. Driving on, the sound of the ocean and the waves breaking on the shore faded into the night behind her.

'Go home, just go back to Perth!' he yelled.

'I can't drive back tonight,' she argued.

'I'm not asking you, I'm telling you! DRIVE! NOW!'

Rattled, she drove the car towards Perth. Fifty kilometres clicked over, the headlights revealed a roadhouse up ahead. Slowing the van down, she turned into the entrance. Anna was taking the petrol cap off when she noticed a stirring inside the van. When the tank was full, the curtains parted and Joe looked outside. She grabbed her wallet and took her last twenty-dollar bill to pay for the petrol. 'I must look a wreck,' she thought to herself, as she walked towards the white fluorescent building.

The smell of grease, cheap coffee, and petrol made her stomach turn. She was too tired to cry. The sleepy attendant by the cash register took the money and Anna heard a noise behind her. The sound of the van's engine turning over startled her. Horrified, she watched the van drive away without her. Not understanding, she waited a minute longer to see if the car was turning around.

'Oh no, Jess! No!' Anna cried to the vacant brightly lit space in front of her.
'My car, the bastard's taking my car.' She screamed at the top of her lungs at the sleepy attendant. He shook his head, confused at her predicament. He looked at his watch—it was twelve thirty in the morning.
'There's only one cop in town.'

'Where's the phone? What's the number?' Anna waived her arms around like a broken puppet. She spoke to the policeman, hysterically reporting what had happened.

When the police car turned up shortly afterwards, it skidded to a halt. The officer inside leaned over towards the passenger window and pushed the passenger door open.
'Get in.'

'You two have a little tiff?' he questioned condescendingly.

'He's drunk and he's driving with our baby in the car!'

'You'll probably laugh about it in the morning,' the policeman joked. Anna thought that the conversation was absurd.

'I don't think so.'

'What do you want me to do then . . . I mean . . . when I pull him over?'

'I want my daughter, Jess safe, and I want my van back and I don't care what happens to him.'

Up ahead the van's taillights came into view. The cop put his siren on. The flashing red light reflected on the expansive black bush on either side of the highway. Grass trees growing abundantly in the fields either side of the road, looked like stranded, stationary people. It sent shivers up Anna's spine. The van pulled to the side of the road and the police car pulled to a halt behind it.

'Hey buddy,' she heard the policeman say to Joe as he walked up to the driver's side window.

'Had a little domestic did we?'

He chatted as he checked the papers and took the keys of the van from Joe. Anna was waiting for the officer to give Joe a breathalyser test—but he didn't.

'Do you want a lift back to town, mate?' The officer asked Joe in a friendly concerned voice.

'No way . . . ah thanks,' replied a surly Joe as he got out of the car.

Anna walked around behind the officer to avoid Joe, grabbed the keys off the policeman and climbing into the van gave Jess a big hug. Relief swept over her.

'Look at the lights Mum,' Jess pointed excitedly at the flashing lights on top of the police car.

'Yes they are bright aren't they?' Anna replied amazed that her daughter was only focused on the lights and not her father.

Starting the engine, she indicated, pulled out from the gravel verge and accelerated forward on the highway. Anna watched Joe get smaller and smaller in the rear view mirror as she drove off. There were no streetlights, only her tail lights heading south and the police car's tail lights heading north and Joe alone, surrounded by grass trees and shadows, getting smaller and smaller in the middle of the night.

Anna turned the radio on to keep herself company; she patted Jess softly of to sleep on the seat beside her. Tracy Chapman was singing:

'You got a fast car, is it fast enough so we can fly away.
We gotta make a decision, do we leave tonight or live and die this way . . .'

She drove for an hour getting as far away from Joe as she could. Her head ached and her eyes were stinging so she pulled over to the side of the road, climbed into the bed in the back and tried to sleep. Her eyes refused to shut. Jess woke up and together they looked at the stars in the night sky and rested.

'Mummy, you know the moon and the stars?'

'Yes,'

'Are they battery operated or what?'

ೲೲೲೲ

Anna didn't understand how you could really call Eneabba a town. It had a shop, a shed, a petrol bowser, and a lone telephone booth. Anna decided to call her mother in Queensland.

'Yes, I'll accept the charges,' she heard her mother say.

'Are you Okay, it's early to be getting a call.'

'No, I'm exhausted, I'm in the middle of nowhere, a place called Eneabba.'

'What are you doing there?'

'Joe got drunk and ruined everything on our holiday.'

'Oh Anna, I'm sure it wasn't that bad.'

'It was worse than bad—I'm so tired of him pulling this shit—I'm leaving him.'

'Well, who's going to look after you then?'

'I'll look after myself—I can't do worse than this.'

'No luv, you need a man to take care of you.'

'You're not hearing me—he's not taking care of me or Jess—he's trying to kill us.'

'Oh Anna, you always exaggerate!'

ଔଔଔଔ

When she got back to Perth, she left him. She found a place in Fremantle for her and Jess to live, a little weatherboard duplex with a small cement courtyard in the front and a huge jacaranda tree in the back. They made a swing for Jess out of an old car tyre. They'd take long walks on the banks of the river. Jess started kindergarten, and riding their bike to school in the mornings was the favourite part of Jess's day. At night, Anna had her bar job behind the bar in Cleo's nightclub.

Spiritual Healing

Anna: I'm afraid of relationships.

Healer: Why do you say that?

Anna: Because every time I get into one my 'lover' wants to kill me. Try and figure that out?

Healer: So how are you creating that for yourself?

Anna: I'm not doing it—they are!

Healer: When you can take responsibility for everything that happens to you in your life and watch out for the clues—you can change it.

Anna: These clues aren't that subtle, more like a Mack truck, I need to fix it quick—I could die if I don't sort this shit out!

Healer: Your unconscious mind is projecting old beliefs onto the present in order for you to heal it. This is a re-action here in your life now from a charged belief in your mind, from the past. It is the answer to a question that quietly guides all of our behaviours in this context. Think about it—What question would you be asking yourself to get this result?

Anna: How am I going to get stabbed in the back this time—how am I going to get hurt . . . yes relationships definitely hurt?

Healer: Excellent. And if you knew what your unconscious mind's positive intention in asking this question is . . . what would that be?

Anna: To keep me safe because my relationships have been dangerous before.

Healer: So knowing now that your unconscious mind can get safety for you; if you had safety already fully and completely and your unconscious mind gets that for you, what even more important thing will you get through that?

Anna: A *Loving* relationship.

Healer: The unconscious is always answering a question for you, so what question do you want answered instead?

Anna: How can I feel loved, nurtured and safe in a relationship?

Healer: How does that feel when you say that out loud?

Anna: It feels really good! But, just as I said that, I saw in my mind the weirdest thing—I became aware that I have this huge sword sticking out of my body and I can't get it out.

Healer: Really! Can you see a sword sticking out of your head?

Anna: I can't see it normally, if you know what I mean. Oh my god you must think I'm crazy—but I can feel it and it has a powerful effect on my life—it shuts me down.

Healer: Who put it there?

Anna: How do I know?

Healer: Close your eyes and go inside and ask yourself.

Anna: What good will that do?

Healer: You can begin to trust yourself. Really—all you need to do is to listen to your inner voice and you will know.

Anna: Okay, when I look inside, my inner vision is showing me that I have this great big metallic sword sticking into my head and it goes down through the centre of my body. It is going through my mind so that I can't think clearly, my thinking is scattered. No it's actually shattered. It feels like my mind has been shattered—it's all over the place, all of the time. This sword goes down into and through my heart so that my heart feels broken and it goes down through my sexuality so that I make bad choices in relationships.

Healer: Does it hurt?

Anna: No but it affects my life—it makes me invisible, it makes nothing I do matter or come to any fruition, so that I have to stay invisible.

Healer: I see, lets take a look at that . . . it's very beautiful, it has a large crystal in the main handle and more precious stones in sections of the handle that are, by the way, protruding out of your ears.

Anna: Great.

Healer: This blade has done a lot of fighting. Many, many battles, not lately if you know what I mean. You are a very old soul and you have fought many battles in other times, you know what I'm saying—in other lifetimes?

Anna: I can see that now, the pictures are flowing into my mind. I put it there, but why would I shut myself down?

Healer: Yes you did put it there. No one can have power over you—spiritually you are always your own authority. Have you ever tried meditating? You will get all of the answers that you need when you go inside yourself.

Anna: I have tried but I've never felt comfortable because I get so scared and freak out and I have to stop.

Healer: What are you scared of?

Anna: I don't know. I just know that it feels terrifying. It feels dangerous—like something terrible is about to happen.

Healer: What is so terrible or dangerous?

Anna: I am dangerous, like I'm too much or something, something inside me is dangerous, *really* dangerous.

Healer: Are you willing to have a look inside and see what is so dangerous? I'll be here for you. I'll hold your hand and go with you if you like.

Anna: I'm terrified and I know that sounds silly because it means that something scary is inside of me and not knowing what that is, that's not good.

Healer: Just relax and know that you have survived everything that has ever happened to you in the past. This is a fear that comes from a past memory, yes?

Anna: I suppose so.

Healer: I want you to relax and imagine a way of going down inside yourself to see what is so scary down there. Talk to me and tell me what you see, so that I can be with you as you go.

Anna: (*closing her eyes*) I see a ladder and it leads down into a tunnel—It's a very long way down—if I had a parachute I could jump, a little like skydiving. No, on second thought, I think I'll take it slowly. The ladder looks strong enough. It's made of thick rope, so thick that I can just manage to hold it with my whole palm and fingers. It feels rough under the skin of my hand.

Healer: How many steps are there? Count us down as you climb down them.

Anna: The first one. I have both feet on it and the rope fits in the middle of my shoe. My footing is good. I'm taking my left foot off the rope and stepping down to the step below and then moving my right foot down also. I'm going to the third step, and now the fourth but I can feel the heat and I can see a red glow. It's very hot down here, you know. I'm feeling very frightened. I don't think that I can do this. I don't think that I can go any further.

Healer: Yes you can. You are doing so well. You are so brave to have come this far and you're nearly there. I'm here with you. Can you feel me holding your hand? This fear is affecting your life. This is your body and now it's time to step past this fear and claim your body back.

Anna: I'm afraid. I can see a big angry monster and he's coming towards me. I've got to get out of here. There are dead bodies here and burning fires, and he's coming to get me.

Healer: I hear you. Now I wonder, when you look into his eyes can you see what he's angry about?

Anna: No I can't. Are you crazy? I'm not going to ask him. I've got to get out of here!

Healer: Just before you do, is he near you now?

Anna: Yes he's very close.

Healer: Good! Just before you come on up, I want you to lean over to him and give him a kiss.

Anna: What!

Healer: Yes stretch your arms out and give that monster a big kiss and a cuddle—See what he does?

Anna: His face is close to mine. *(In that instant, she hugs the monster and in her arms it transforms into a huge brightly coloured Dragon. He's lime green and lavender and yellow and orange. He takes off with Anna holding on tightly around his neck.)* 'Wow where is he taking me?' *The dragon soars upward out into the universe.*

'Whoah! I'm flying!' squealed Anna holding on tightly to her dragon's neck. 'He's swirling and turning and flying at the speed of light,' laughed Anna, hanging on for her life.

Anna sat back in the chair, her breath was rapid and full, her eyes were closed and behind her eyelids in her mind she experienced the trip of her life, into the void, across the abyss and eventually back into the present and into the room. Her dragon settles down with her in her comfortable seat, next to the Healer. The dragon stays close by and waits for the session to be over.

Anna drove home in a daze. She curled up on her bed in the middle of the day and fell into a deep and comfortable sleep. In her dreams she noticed that her dragon was beside her on the bed. She was lying under one of his wings in the crevice of his belly and nestling her head on one of his tummy rolls. She felt content and protected. The hole that held the monster and the fear, was now filled with the rainbow lights of her dragon, the demon had been transformed.

The following week Anna went back to the Healer for another session.

Healer: How are you?

Anna: I feel wonderful. I've been sleeping!

I don't think that I could ever sleep as a child. I was always on an adrenalin rush because I was worried that something terrible was going to happen when I was asleep. I was always hyper vigilant.

My dragon has been protecting me and I have been sleeping, and it feels delicious.

Healer: A good question for you to answer for yourself might be: *Is trust in yourself dependent on others?*

Husband II

He came into the bar one night. He was tall, handsome and happy with himself. Their conversation was easy and fun. Shane was his name and he was confident that he liked her. 'Want to go to the movies sometime?' he asked on his way out.

'No thanks,' she'd said. But the next day she bumped into him at the coffee shop and later that night she saw him at the movies.

'We did get to go to the movies after all,' he joked.

A few weeks later at a party on a Saturday night they met again.

'*Hey beaudiful, we meet again,*' he said, leaning over and kissing her on the cheek. He'd been at the party longer than Anna and it showed.

'I've had too much to drink tonight, but I'm going to call you. You have to come over and see my rock collection.'

※ ※ ※ ※

He invited her back to his house to see his rock collection. His house was the strangest renovation she'd ever seen, and it wasn't finished. A spiral staircase went down to a sitting room where a large part of the wall was missing.

'I'm going to put French doors in there, but I haven't got around to it yet,' he said casually.

A six-foot high sandstone wall enclosed a garden, which was also partly finished.

'I work away in the mining industry and when I come home I build this place,' he told her.

After a tour of the house they came back upstairs to the lounge room. It was empty except for an old red leather lounge, a sound system, still partially in its box and a battered, brown suitcase. The floors were pine boards, simple and elegant. High, pressed tin ceilings gave the room the feel of a cathedral.

'This is my collection,' he said, laying the case on its side and opening the lid. There were opals and rocks, shards of shale, natural silver and gold. The biggest one caught her eye, a perfect heart shape. It looked heavy, but it was as light as a pebble. It was black and cold in the palm of her hand.

'That's my heart, it's volcanic,' he said.

'It's cold,' she said, swapping it quickly for another.

Some felt ancient in her hands and they were all different. Most of the rocks from Shane's collection were from the earth's surface, but others came from deep down underneath it. One sample was from the inside of a drilling bit, one hundred meters beneath the desert, near Halls Creek. He'd cut the rock diagonally to reveal the leaf of a fern tree, a perfect fossil.

'You really do have a rock collection!' she said, smiling as he handed her a Corona beer.

They had a few drinks together and the evening passed pleasantly. He leaned forward and touched her face with one hand and gently pulled her to him with the other.

His face touched hers and they both felt an electrical shock, like a shock she sometimes got off the shopping trolley or the car door. She jumped backwards and giggled. 'Whoa! That was different,' she laughed.

Shane walked her back to her house and he came in for a while. They were kissing on the sofa when there was a knock on the door.

'Anna, I know you're in there.'

'Who's that?' Shane asked.

'It's my ex, we've been separated for months, but sometimes he bashes on my door in the middle of the night,' said Anna feeling stupid and embarrassed.

'I have a restraining order, but they are not worth the paper that they are printed on.' Anna added.

'Do you want me to sort it out?'

'No, he'll go away if we ignore it.'

They sat a while and the noise outside subsided. Shane pulled her into his arms,

'I'll never hurt you Anna,' he said, as he squeezed her tight.

❦❦❦❦

Shane was good with Jess. He'd pluck blues tunes on his guitar and she would sing along. Jess asked him to read to her at night but instead he would recite his favourite poem.

'The time has come, the Walrus said,
To talk of many things:
Of shoes and ships and sealing wax—
Of cabbages and kings—
And why the sea is boiling hot-
And whether pigs have wings.'

Anna thought, 'Alice in Wonderland, how cute!'

❦❦❦❦

Jess was turning five. Anna thought that a child's birthday party should be pretty easy to organise, especially since kids just want to have fun. It should be like a chemical reaction, a synaptic response to party food and balloons. Pin the tail on the donkey went well except for Jess continually peeking out from under the blindfold looking towards the front door, expecting her father Joe to ring the doorbell. The guests sang 'Happy Birthday,' a little too loudly. Lolly bags were handed out quickly, trying to sweeten the moment. The cake was an elephant shape covered with fluffy pink icing. Liquorice toe—nails, banana lolly tusks, and a red confectionary snake made a tail. The brightly coloured fairy bread tasted like brittle black beads in between Anna's teeth.

Deflated balloons shifted across the dark wooden floorboards as the guests opened the front door to leave. The house was dim. The duplex briefly held the vanishing light of sunset as the last friend said goodbye. Jess turned to her mother with tears in her big blue eyes.

'Why didn't he come mum?'

Anna didn't know. 'Why?' No matter how much work she had done to make it a special day, Jess's fifth birthday was spoiled. He always promised to be there, but he never was. Looking to Shane for support, she kept silent. Shane opened the fridge and took out a beer as if it would help him explain. Pulling up a chair, he sat back at the kitchen table and took a long slow mouthful of cold ale.

'Ah honey . . . come over here,' he spoke in a calm, confident way, pulling Jess onto his lap.

'Your dad loves ya sweet-heart, he just doesn't know how to show it.'

He lifted her up onto the table so that she was facing him. 'Your mummy and me are gunna get married and you're gunna have a little brother or sister. We're gunna be a real family.'

Jess didn't say anything. She looked to her mother who was pouring herself a drink. She nervously put her fingers into her mouth. The texture of her teeth was smooth and slippery and she clenched her jaw tight.

'You've had a nice party, its bedtime. Clean your teeth and get to bed.' Shane said patting Jess gently on the backside as she walked off towards her bedroom.

Jess had been asleep for about an hour when the doorbell rang. Anna's hair was wrapped in a towel, still wet from the shower. Shane had cleared the main mess but there was still evidence of the party. Anna kicked her toe on Jess's toy stroller on the way to the door. Swearing under her breath, she opened it, and the smell of stale beer, spirits and smoke hit her in the face. Joe looked old and agitated. His smooth brown skin looked rough and blotchy, like an old piece of toast. His hair was a wild mess of black ringlets and it hung down over his wrinkled forehead. He was shorter than Anna by an inch or so and that bothered him. She met his glance but then he looked down at the floor.

'I've lost my licence again,' he mumbled under his breath and nudged his way past her, heading through the lounge room to the kitchen.

'What?' said Anna.

Shane was seated at the table having a cigarette.

'The party's over Joe,' he announced loudly as he reached forward for the bottle of bourbon and made himself a drink.

'I was in lock up. I couldn't make it. Six hundred dollar fine and my licence suspended for six months.'

'You didn't have a licence to lose,' said Anna.

'I know. That's why it's six hundred dollars.'

'What about your job?'

'I don't want to think about it—can I have one of those Shane,' he motioned to the bourbon bottle.

'I could really use a drink. I'm gunna have to sell my Ute . . .'

Shane poured him a few good inches of liquid and Joe topped it up with coke from the large glass bottle on the table.

'How did you get here?' Anna asked.

'I walked.'

'How are you getting home?'

'I'll walk. I'm just having one for the road.'

Anna turned away and left the room. She went and sat by the fire to warm herself and dry her hair. Sitting on the floor she tried to sit up straight and roll her tight shoulders; she reached forward to stretch her aching muscles. Her stomach fluttered. She brushed her long hair and waited nervously for him to leave.

The stilted conversation in the kitchen stumbled awkwardly from cars to football and then Anna heard Jess's name mentioned. Voices became tense. She heard a whack, then a loud thud. Jumping to her feet, she rushed into the kitchen. Shane sat at the table, upright but staggering. In that frozen moment, Shane's forehead showed indentations and raised furrows. Pulsing like a Coca Cola sign, the skin on his forehead swelled letters. Joe held the heavy coke bottle in his hand, intact. Jess loved taking them back to the shop for a five-cent refund.

'What happened?' Anna questioned, 'Did you hit him, Joe?'

The look on Shane's face changed, suddenly violet, his lips curled out like a purple gourmet lettuce. His eyes bulged, bloodshot in their sockets. He lunged forward, grabbing Joe's throat, clenching his neck with one hand before he smashed his other fist into Joe's face.

Anna screamed as their bodies knocked her aside and crashed through a wall. Shane picked Joe up with the force of fury and smashed him into another wall, demolishing it as well. Anna doubled over feeling sick. She stopped screaming when she remembered that Jess was asleep in the front room. It crossed her mind to call the police but she just sat there, immobile, looking at them—wild bodies, fists and feet. Joe made a guttural sound as Shane pinned his head up against the wall. His feet dangled in the air beneath him.

Anna ran into Jess's room. Somehow she was still sleeping. Anna sat on the side of her little daughter's bed and started to cry.

In the morning, Jess came into the kitchen looking for breakfast and Anna was up at the table having a coffee, trying to ignore the damage to her house.

'My dad's a good fighter,' she announced.

A blanket of despair came over Anna as she walked to the phone booth down the road, dialled the operator and asked for a collect-call to her mother.

'Yes, I'll accept the charges,' she heard her mother say.

'Hello.'

'Hi, Anna, how are you.'

'No good, Joe came over and started a fight with Shane. He destroyed my house.'

'Oh, that's no good luv.'

'He was drunk and he missed Jess's party.'

'Oh Anna, you know what they're like. When a man works hard all week, he just wants time to relax, not go to a kid's birthday party. I'm sure he didn't mean it.'

※ ※ ※ ※

Shane and Anna decided to leave Perth and find a place in the country. They found a property near the Porongorup National Park that needed management. The Porongurup National Park covers 2,511 hectares. The granite domes of Porongurup National Park rise over the plain 40 kilometres north of Albany. Twelve kilometres long and 670 metres at its highest point, the Porongurup Range is renowned for its beauty. The granite from which the Porongurup Range is formed is more than 1,100 million years old, and at first Anna felt overwhelmed and frightened to be there.

The homestead was a rambling three-bedroom house with a number of sheds. The large kitchen had a combustion stove and some odd pieces of furniture: A pine sideboard with brass handles, a dining table with carved legs, an old cast iron kettle with a long curved spout, and a solid oak table with two long pews.

Kangaroos grazed in the paddocks every day. Each morning and evening, a sunrise or a sunset could take your breath away as the light fell on Bluff Knoll. The property was run down, but the views from every window were spectacular and the living room had a huge fireplace that added to the charm and character of the place.

The hot water system was broken. Frayed insulation lay on the ground around the base of the heater. Shane got to work at first light, doing whatever repairs he could. Anna collected some firewood and mallee roots and they were both surprised to find that the heater worked efficiently.

Whoever had lived in the house previously had painted a huge mural on the walls in the lounge room. Red and yellow flames flickered; black bodies were depicted falling to their deaths in what seemed to be damnation. It was an ugly picture and it gave Anna the creeps. She wondered who had drawn them, as she scrubbed them away with sugar soap as quickly as she could.

One summer day at Mt Barker swimming pool, a local woman with curly, red hair and the biggest freckles Anna had ever seen, asked:
'Are you a blow in?'
'What's a blow in?'
'Oh—once I made friends with one an she up and left town after a cupla years!'
'Well, I think I must be one of them.' Anna smiled.
'You livin in *that* house?' she queried.
'We live in the Porongurups.'

'Yeah, *that* house! . . . 1107, Johnny Chester lived there ya know, he blew up the Bunbury woodchip factory, so they'd stop woodchippen.'

'Did it work?' asked Anna.

'No they just built nuther one, but lader, Chester chained himself to a tree.'

'Why?'

'He wanted to fast for fordy days like Christ did!'

'Did he make it?'

'No, he didn't. Only, while he was chained up—his wife packed up the kids and took off!'

Waist deep in water, Anna tried not to smile at the woman's animated story. She pulled herself and her growing belly out of the water and reached for her sarong. The local woman reached into her bag on the side of the pool and pulled out a packet of Winfield Blue cigarettes.

'Want a smoke?' she said, offering Anna one.

'No thanks.'

'Suit yourself,' she said taking a long drag on her cigarette and then a sip of coke and added, 'The abos won't stay out there after dark, neither. Reckon you could get turned to stone.'

૭૦૭૦૭૦૭૦

Despite the warnings from the locals and the complete isolation of the property, with the nearest neighbour four kilometres away, Anna was feeling happy and strong. Sometimes for no apparent reason she found herself singing. She sat down on the veranda, looking out at sunrise over the Stirling Ranges and pulled on her dusty black gum boots. The elastic waistband of her baggy trousers stretched around her large belly. Moving with more of a waddle than a walk, stoking the fire, feeding animals, spinning wool, cooking, hanging out the washing, she surprised herself with how content she had become.

The city girl mellowed and it felt good to settle in her skin. The Porongurup sunrise nourished her with peaceful colour, and the big round balls of granite rock looked like giant marbles. Each day began softly, with her calm breath meeting the steam off her morning cup of tea. Kangaroos grazed on the grass outside her kitchen window. By eight fifteen each morning, she'd done some yoga, had breakfast, seen Shane off to work and walked her five-year old daughter up to the school bus.

Anna was comfortable being alone now. She wore baggy trousers and dashing black gumboots that came up to her knees. Anna completed her outfit by grabbing Shane's woollen jacket off the peg by the backdoor. She took her cup of tea out onto the veranda. Holding her right arm up, she shook her shoulder into the jacket. Snow covered the top of Bluff Knoll in the distance and the icy morning wind made her nipples freeze before she had time to pull the jacket around herself. She shivered. 'Can I have it this good?' she thought.

Reclaiming The Child

*A*nna *was sitting comfortably in a soft three-seater lounge, feeling a little nervous. She was glad that her husband, Shane had come along with her to the meditation. Even though they had their problems, he was sometimes open to new things.*

'Everyone take a seat and get yourself comfortable.' Deborah introduced herself and began the workshop. 'This workshop is all about you and reclaiming and championing aspects of your inner child.'

'Today's meditation will be focusing on the toddler self—These courses have come from John Bradshaw's work—'Homecoming'—Bradshaw believed that in order to understand your true self—you need to understand your inner self and the family system that you come from. Bradshaw also believed that if you don't know your family history you are very likely to repeat it.'

'This isn't going to go well.' Shane whispered into Anna's ear.

Anna felt a sinking feeling in her stomach but she sat up a little straighter and looked up to the front of the room.

'Let's begin today with a meditation.'

Anna closed her eyes and she was noticing her breathing and listening to the meditation; she felt safe with Shane sitting on the floor near by. She felt comfortable with him close to her and she felt herself begin to relax into the soft cushions of the couch.

'Relax your eyes and all of the muscles around your eyes . . . fully and completely and notice your breathing and become aware how the breath touches

your lungs and notice the sides of your lungs and wander deeply into calm and comfort.' Deborah said.

'Where else can you breathe into if you don't breathe into your lungs!' said Shane elbowing Anna jokingly.
'Shane!' whispered Anna, 'Please, cut it out!'

'Start by sitting quietly and becoming aware of your surroundings . . . locate yourself in space and time. Feel your back and bottom touching the chair you're sitting in . . . feel your clothes on your body . . .'

'Well you couldn't feel them if they were off your body,' remarked Shane sarcastically under his breath.

'Hear as many different sounds as you can hear . . . feel the air in the room . . . Just for now, there's no place you have to be, nobody wanting anything and nothing for you to do except relax . . . just breathing deeply and feeling the air as it comes in and goes out . . . Your breath may have a healing colour . . .'

'The colour of shit,' whispered Shane, laughing out loud at his own joke.
'This could be your favourite soft colour as you breathe in and out.'
'Soft shit,' said Shane snickering to himself up the back of the room.
'Allowing any thoughts to just fade away, like the bubbles in a glass of lemonade just allow the thoughts to rise to the top of your mind and pop into nothing . . .'
Deborah continued.
'Pop a few pills is what I need to do if I have to listen to any more of this shit!' Shane said.
'Hey babe, please give it a chance!' Anna pleaded rubbing his shoulders gently.

'Relaxing more and more as you notice how relaxed you're becoming, as you feel a heaviness in your head and face, and down the shoulders, and arms and hands, letting go of tension . . . Notice the most relaxed muscle in your body, and

Reclaiming Trust

then another muscle somehow more relaxed . . . all the way down through your whole body and you may feel that same relaxed heaviness in your legs and in your feet . . . a heaviness, a tingling feeling, or a lightness it is really up to you . . . whatever feels right for the comfort of you . . . and now you begin experiencing some childhood memories . . . you can remember the house you lived in before you went to school . . . what colour was the house ? . . . Was it an apartment? . . . Now spend some time in the rooms of that house . . .

Did you have a special room? Where was the dinner table? . . . See who's at the dinner table . . . what did it feel like to be at the table?

'Arrrggh,' Shane was groaning on the floor. 'My parents didn't like me very much!' he said cringing with pain.

Anna tried to ignore Shane—she could see herself little, maybe four years old, standing on a chair by the stove, talking to her Granny. In her memory she was at her own house and her grandmother was minding her. Maybe she was helping her cooking. Anna felt like she told her something, but she couldn't remember what it was. Suddenly, she felt nervous and then she felt sick. Granny grabbed her hand and pushed it onto the stove burning her fingers.

'You shut your mouth and don't you dare tell a soul!' Anna remembered Granny saying to her, and she felt shocked and terrified.

'Let yourself feel whatever you feel, whatever is there . . . and then imagine the grown up 'adult you' going in and getting the 'little you.' Hear him or her assure you that they will never leave you and that from now on, they will always be available to you.'

Anna could hear Shane coughing. She opened her eyes for a moment and she saw him dry retching and frothing at the mouth.

'Tell your little inner child—I've prepared you a special place for you to live. Your needs are okay with me. I will listen to you.' Deborah advised the group.

'. . . Gently begin to come back to the present moment, to once again becoming your grown up self . . . look at your precious little toddler self . . . be aware that you have reclaimed her or him . . . feel the sense of homecoming . . . that little toddler is wanted, loved, and will never be alone again . . . Walk out of that room, out of that house, and look back as you walk away. Stroll forward up memory lane . . . Walk into early adult memory. Now walk into where you are right now . . . feel your toes and wiggle them . . . feel the energy come up through your legs . . . feel the energy in your chest . . . as you take a deep breath. Make a noise as you exhale . . . feel the energy in your arms and fingers . . . wiggle your fingers . . . feel the energy in your shoulders, neck and jaw . . . stretch your arms. Feel your face and be fully present . . . be fully restored to your normal waking consciousness . . . and open your eyes.

'How would you trust that you had healed the past completely? Now take a moment to allow yourself to reflect on the experience you've just had.'

Anna was curled up on the couch and she could see Shane curled up on the floor beneath her.

'How was that?' Anna whispered to Shane.

'That was fucked, that's how that was! My father hit me around the head with a pool cue when I was eight!'

'Why'

'What do you mean why? When would there ever be a reason to hit a kid around the head with a pool cue!'

'My grandmother burned my hand on the stove.' Anna said in a monotone voice.

'What the fuck? Talk about getting someone when they're down.'

'I was so little.'

'That is absolutely gutless to hurt a little kid like that.'

'I suppose they did the best they could'

'Well it wasn't fucking good enough!' Shane said wrapping his arms around Anna hugging her close.

Shane and Anna left the group and went to the local shopping centre. People walked quickly past them as they both wandered slowly window-shopping. The lights seemed very bright to Anna. Maybe her eyes were a little sensitive from crying at the workshop. Maybe coming to a shopping centre wasn't the best idea; they'd been hungry, but now that they were here they weren't hungry after all. They walked into a toy store and Anna picked up a huge teddy bear and hugged it close to her breast. It felt so soft that she didn't want to put it down.

'I had one just like this when I was little.'
'Can I help you?' the shop assistant enquired politely.
'Only mine had a zipper in the back.'
'We will have that bear,' Shane said taking his wallet out of his back pocket and wrapping his arms around Anna pulling her close to him again.

They arrived at Merrin's house to visit.
'What's with the teddy?' Merrin asked as soon as she saw them.
'I saw it in the shops and Shane bought it for me.'
'It's just like the one I bought for you before I went away to hospital, you wouldn't remember, you were only two years old.'

ତ ତ ତ ତ

Living in the Porongurups, had been good for Anna and she knew it. When they'd first moved to the country to live in the farmhouse, Anna remembered how fearful of snakes she had been... It was night. Pitch black bush, and the brightest sky full of stars that she had ever seen. That had been nine months ago. She had made Shane point the headlights of the car at the front of the house, so that she could walk in the pathway of light to the front door without encountering any snakes. Anna had sneaked along, lifting her feet high with each step and eyes on overdrive, focusing and scanning the ground. Now her fear of snakes had subsided.

One morning she'd awaken and the fields would be the colour purple and a few days later those same fields, would be covered with a quilt of pink or yellow. Native Australian wild flowers became her favourite flowers. As the days turned into weeks she thought less and less about fearful things and more about the beauty of nature.

ତ ତ ତ ତ

The Ducati 1100 purred down the driveway. Shane had finally found some work at a neighbouring property, doing fencing. The bike pulled up outside the house and Anna heard big boot footsteps, then felt his arms wrapping around her from behind and his prickly beard rub against the back of her neck. She loved his hugs. Even with her belly, their bodies felt comfortable together and she turned and embraced him.

'Hey, sweetheart, how are you?' he asked.

His husky male tones were as warm as an old blanket. His hands rested on her stomach.

'This is how I love you, barefoot and pregnant,' he said jokingly, bending forward to speak into her belly. 'Hello beautiful, not long 'til I see you!'

Pulling away, she reached for the bread and started making some lunch. Shane put some music on. 'Way out West,' James Blundell and James Reyne echoed through the house and across the green fields as they ate their lunch. Shane rolled himself a joint and talked about his morning. He seemed happy and animated. His green eyes sparkled when he smiled. Shane hadn't shaved, he was covered in dirt and he looked great. 'How is that possible?' Anna thought to herself as she watched him closely.

'There's lots of work on, three months, guaranteed!' he announced proudly.

'We're gunna be okay,' he said. 'Why don't you have a rest?'

'That sounds good, my back is aching a little.'

'I have to go into town,' he told her casually. 'Jess can come with me.'

'That's a great idea,' she said kissing him as she walked past, heading for the bedroom.

Anna was laying down resting on the bed when she heard the bike engine turn over. Anna sat upright. Trying to get to her feet quickly, she felt her back muscles strain. She'd assumed that he would take the car.

'Oh no, Shane, it's too far,' she mumbled to herself, knowing that he couldn't hear her.

When she looked out the window she could see that Jess was excited, she was clapping her hands together as he lifted her up to the back of his bike.

'No Shane, not the bike,' she yelled.

Frantically, Anna looked for the car keys. She wanted to catch them before they got to the gate at the top of the driveway. Finding the keys in the kitchen and supporting her stomach with one hand, she waddled as fast as she could to the van. Squeezing her belly behind the steering wheel, she started the engine and skidded up the gravel driveway. Shane turned left onto the bitumen and rode towards Mt Barker with Jess perched behind him, hanging on tight.

Anna accelerated, intending to catch up to him. She put her foot down on the pedal and the engine responded. She was making ground, catching up, when suddenly the screaming sound of splitting steel exploded from underneath the bonnet. It sounded fatal. Steam and smoke wafted out, filling the cabin, and the car slowed and rolled to a halt. Anna managed to steer it to the side of the road before it stopped all together.

'Great,' she said to herself. 'Now what am I going to do!'

There was nothing for her to do now but wait for them to come back.

Anna waited for more than half an hour. Pictures of her being rushed to hospital to deliver her child on the back of the Shane's Ducati flashed through her mind.

Finally she saw the bike coming towards her in the distance. Returning from town Shane spotted the car and sped up to it . . . worried that she might be in labour.

'What's wrong, is it time?' he asked. Jess peeped around from behind Shane with a big smile on her face.

'I'm okay! I just didn't want Jess to go on the bike. She's too little!'

'Jess was fine with me, don't you know I'd never let anything happen to her?'

'I just didn't want to risk it Shane, she's little.'

Shane was silent for a moment.

'Why don't you trust me?'

'It's not that Shane, I just think that she's too little to take on the bike.'

'Now what are we going to do?'

He lit up a cigarette and drew the smoke deep into his lungs, like a dragon holding back his fire, and finally, breathing it out of both nostrils and flicking the butt into the bush.

Anna sat alone while Shane rode Jess home.

'It's not my fault. Maybe the motor would have blown next time we drove it anyway,' she stated when Shane came back to pick her up.

'We have no phone, a baby due any day and now, no car and no money to fix it!' he snarled.

He motioned for her to get on. When they arrived back at the house he stayed on his bike.

'I'm going to see if I can borrow a car,' he said as he lifted the visor on his helmet.

Anna saw the look in his eyes, and she knew that he was angry as he rode off.

He was gone for hours. It got dark. Anna had dinner with Jess, and they were in the bathroom when they finally heard the sound of a car in the driveway.

'Shane's back mum,' Jess squealed jumping up to dry herself and put her pyjamas on. She raced happily to the front door to greet him.

'Get to bed!' he snapped at her as he came through the door.

Anna pulled herself out of the water and wrapped a towel around her body.

'Why?' asked Jess. 'It's not bedtime yet.'

'Because I said so,' he said, smashing his fist on the kitchen table.

Anna rushed into the room, to see Jess running to her room. She was shocked at his tone, until she smelt him.

'What's wrong?' she asked as she came into the lounge room.

'What's wrong?' he mocked her.

His eyes were bloodshot. Anna turned her face away from his alcoholic breath.

'What dooya think is wrong, ya stupid bitch?'

'What is happening?' Anna thought to herself. She slowly moved towards the bedroom to get some clothes. As she moved past him, he ripped the towel off her leaving her naked and vulnerable. She took a few steps backward. He picked up a handful of plums from the kitchen table and threw them at her.

Anna tried to duck and weave away but they hurtled through the air, pelting her breasts and belly. Plums punctuated his anger. Trying to protect herself, she went for the bedroom and attempted to shut the door. He pushed the door open and she fell backwards onto the bed. Anna looked up into his angry twisted face and she wondered how this could be happening to her? She watched the muscles around his mouth contort as he yelled at her.

'Who do you think you are?' He roared at her.

'I ride that bike like a professional and I would never hurt Jess. I've never given you reason not to trust me!' he screamed.

The veins in the side of his neck pulsed and protruded to the beat of his words.

Anna had always thought that if she could mend something it would last longer. She was committed to making a happy home. Mothering was important to her. Sunshine shining in on the kitchen table: fairy outfits and stories at bedtime. Brilliant colours, homemade curtains and pillows to brighten things up. Anna was always trying to brighten things up. She'd learnt that from her mother a long time ago, but tonight, Anna knew that this was broken.

Shane worked hard—she knew that! Twelve-hour days were minimum on the farming roster, regardless of the weather. It could get so hot in the summer that new guys on the job would pass out from heat exhaustion. He told her that he'd drink ten litres of water a day and never had to take a piss. He was really proud of that. He was bronze and fit, and hard as a piece of wire. When he came home from work he was always covered in the fine brown dust that made up the land that he worked on.

As she stood up, he picked the end of the bed up and flipped it over. He put his fist through the window in the bedroom sending splintered glass everywhere. Shane stood in the doorway boxing her in. Anna thought she was hallucinating: she backed up against the wall as he pushed his face into hers.

'I'm so angry, I could kill you,' he said.

Fleetingly, she thought she saw her father's face and then Joe's face, flicker across Shane's face. Shane took a deep breath. He looked at his bleeding hand.

'Now, look what you've done!' he breathed through clenched teeth, into her face.

'Me? You did it! What happened to—I'll never hurt you Anna?'

'You tall, stroppy, bitch, I haven't hurt you—YET!' he threatened, standing over her.

Shane shook his head in pain and torment and then he glared at her. It happened again in an instant, for a fleeting second, she thought she saw her father's angry face floating in the air between them. She realised in that split second, *somehow,* she'd made this happen.

Shane went to get another drink and stop his hand bleeding. Anna frantically grabbed a T—shirt and some track pants. She walked barefoot over the glass to get to Jess's room, and whispered for her to lock the door and wait by her window.

'We have to leave here, in a minute! Get a jacket and shoes on.'

Anna was trying to dress herself. She could see Shane sitting at the kitchen table, calm for a moment. He took a long swig of beer from the can and sat quietly.

When he did talk, Anna thought he was joking. 'I'm going to kill us, first you and Jess and then myself,' Shane said soberly. Anna laughed a little at the absurdity of his words whilst searching to make sense of this craziness, and pulling on her track pants.

'You are over reacting! What's really the matter?' she pleaded with him pulling on a T-shirt and thinking how she was going to get Jess and herself out of there. She knew he had guns. He wasn't *that* drunk. She knew that he could drink like a fish. Unfortunately, Shane didn't look like he was joking.

'Shane, don't be ridiculous,' she said, finding her thongs under the table and slipping them onto her feet.

'I have a lot of living to do and so has Jess. So keep us out of your brilliant plan.'

Over the few years that they had been married Shane had told her snippets from his life as a child. He had never felt loved by his parents. His father, Jack had been a prisoner of war in Germany for four years. He was captured on his very first mission; he'd parachuted over enemy lines and on landing, impaled himself on a sharp fence post that pierced through his leg. Jack never got to fire his gun. He'd felt like a failure, a dud, a shell of a soldier.

The only exploding Jack ever did was his fits of rage, years later, around his little boys. He shot his pain into his children. Shane told Anna stories of his mother too. One time when he wouldn't eat his dinner, she hit his head against the wall until it made a hole in the plaster.

Shane told Anna that his parents would go off to parties and leave him and his little brother Noah at their step-brother, Carlos's house. Carlos was twelve years older than Shane. The two boys hated being at Carlos' place *so much*. A few times Shane had forced Noah to eat a bar of Sunshine velvet soap *'gentle on your hands and everything they wash.'* When Noah started vomiting, they got to go home.

Anna got up to leave the room and to check if Jess was all right, but he grabbed her and pushed her into the kitchen bench. He put one hand around her throat and with the other Shane picked up a knife from the knife block on the kitchen bench and shoved it up to her face.

'It's okay Jess,' Anna shakily called to her daughter, 'Mummy's coming to get you in a minute.' Anna clenched Shane's hand trying to release his grip.

When she'd won that set of knives in the local pub raffle, they'd given a demonstration on how sharp they were. It was the first time

Anna had ever won anything. He hit her. He'd never actually hit her before.

Reeling backwards and covering her stomach with one hand, trying to protect herself and her unborn baby, Anna looked around the kitchen thinking about her exit. Shane was telling her now, how he was going to get his gun.

'Why is this happening to me?' was the only thing that Anna kept thinking. She was in shock, she was terrified but it was so crazy—so ridiculous that she couldn't think straight. She knew that she didn't want to die. She looked at the glass sliding door leading out to the front yard and, as Shane was saying, 'Don't even think about doing a runner.'

She was off, electrified with fear. She slid the sliding door back and bolted through the doorway.

Shane was right behind her and she noticed her hand, still on the door handle. Anna pulled it shut in a fluid movement. It surprised her how it rolled to a close in slow motion as his face, head and his angry, awkward body smashed into the other side of the thick pane of glass and then fell hard onto the floor. Anna let out a nervous giggle. Shaking, she pulled herself together and raced up the path to the garden gate. She could hear him coming close behind her again and rushing, grabbed the handle of the wooden gate too hard and took the skin off her knuckles. Anna opened the gate a little and slid through the narrow space. The gate blocked Shane's way and she was through—into the bushes, into the darkness, and out of his sight.

'Anna, get back here!' Shane shouted into the darkness, as if he expected her to come back. He stopped and stood still for the longest moment and then turned and walked back into the house.

Anna sprinted around to the other side of the house to Jess's bedroom; she slid the window back and saw Jess crying, standing behind her bedroom door. Jess had locked the door shut.

'Good girl Jess, grab your shoes and come quickly!'
'Mummy, what's happening?'
'We have to leave now.' Anna grabbed her daughter, lifted her over the windowsill and slipped into the night with Jess on her hip. Somehow her body moved quickly. She had always been an athlete, a runner, and she knew that he could not catch her now. Anna spirited through the bush up to the dark road like the wind was part of her. On reaching the road, she crouched down hugging her stomach and her unborn child with Jess close by her side. Stopping quietly, barely breathing, Anna looked behind her to check if he had followed.

The lights on the front porch shone and then a spotlight scanned the bush land around the house. Anna and Jess huddled together in the dark, ducking their heads down behind the bushes. Anna could feel blood running in between her fingers. She felt a stinging pain on her knuckles. Her feet were hurting too, and somehow she had lost her thongs. The car that Shane had borrowed started up in the driveway, and headed towards town.

Squatting in the dirt, Anna and Jess froze. They saw the lights again, heard the engine speeding back past them, heading in the opposite direction toward Albany. When the headlights had faded and the motor could only be heard in the distance, mother and daughter emerged holding hands. They walked together towards help. The closest neighbour was kilometres away. Anna's feet were tender already. High in the night sky, the full moon and the stars lit the road ahead of them.

'Mummy, why does this happen to us?' Jess asked.
'I don't know honey. Somehow I think it's me.'
'No mum, I know—men hate women and women hate men!'
'Oh Jess, no.'
'But I love the moon and the stars, mum.'
'I love you, Jess.'

Much later, walking along the driveway of her neighbour's house, a wave of relief washed over Anna and she squeezed Jess's hand tight.

Just like his father, Shane had passed his pain onto his children.

'No more,' Anna thought to herself. Sometimes when something is broken it is best to throw it away.

Anna and Jess walked hand in hand. Anna felt shaken but confident that she would hear a car coming in either direction, so they took it easy and tried to relax into the night.

They arrived at Deb's house at midnight and knocked on the door.

'What on earth?' Deb said, when she answered the door half asleep.

'We've had a drama, and we need some help,' Anna said feeling ashamed of her situation.

'Oh my god, you both look terrible! Come in and let's get you comfortable—you can't be having drama with this beautiful girl,' she said, giving Jess a big squeeze and pulling her into the house. 'Or this beautiful baby in here,' she said, giving Anna and her huge tummy a hug.

'Oh how lovely!' said Anna collapsing into the recliner in the living room.

'You're bleeding!' Deb said in despair.

'I took the skin off my knuckles closing the gate in a hurry to get away.'

'Hurry to get away from what?'

'Shane! He had some sort of meltdown, breakdown . . . definitely a freak out!'

'What's that mark on you cheek and you have marks all over your neck!'

'Yes that's where he tried to strangle me . . . kill me, kill us . . . what do you call that except completely unacceptable and scary and insane?'

'Assault! That's what that is. I'll take you to the police station—he should be charged.'

'Okay, in the morning.'

'My goodness, you should go to the hospital.'

'No, I feel exhausted, I need to rest.'

'You'll go to the doctor. I can take you now to the hospital.'

'No I'm fine. And I couldn't handle that now!'

'Then first thing in the morning we're going to the doctor. I'll make you some tea and I've cooked some scones. And tomorrow we'll fix everything and you can go for a swim in the heated pool Jess and we'll have a lovely day.'

'Can I go for a swim now?' Jess asked.

'Okay—it looks very warm—let's go for a swim.'

Anna and Deb sat in the comfortable poolside chairs having tea and scones while they watched Jess floating on her back in the water.

'Look at the stars mum. Look how big the moon is.'

'It's beautiful my darling, just like you.'

'Come in and swim with me, the water is warm, it feels good.'

'Oh honey, I don't think I can.'

'Please, mum.'

'Maybe that would make me feel better,' she said to Deb.

'I have some warm clean clothes when you get out.'

'Hold on I'm coming in,' said Anna to Jess as she lowered herself into the water in her clothes. She swam over to her little daughter, holding her close and kissing her cheek.

'This is just perfect Deb,' said Anna feeling very grateful to be safe.

'Girls, I don't understand,' Deb said, with a confused frown. 'How could this happen to you? You're so loveable Anna, and you don't deserve this violent angry behaviour. Not tonight. Not ever.'

'It was so weird, when it was happening, when Shane was threatening me with his fist in my face, I saw Joe's face with the same expression and then Harry's face. It was like somehow I've been creating this situation over and over again.'

Uncle

Anna's uncle Ken was her father's little brother. Harry was taller and stronger than Ken. Harry played football better than him. In fact, he played all sports better than his brother. Harry didn't intentionally make him feel bad, it just happened that way. Ken always felt small around Harry and before he knew it, before Ken had time to figure out what he was good at, or what he was meant to be—he had a few drinks to drown his sorrows, and drowning his sorrows became the thing that Ken did best.

Ken drank every day, and each day he drank a little more. Harry wanted to help him snap out of it—so they planned a holiday away in the country. Ken was drunk when Harry suggested the trip. Ken was drunk when they packed the car. By the time he sobered up Harry was driving. Merrin, Tess, and Anna were all in the back seat.

They had been driving all day without incident and then right on dusk, just twenty kilometres away from their final destination, Forbes, they hit a kangaroo. The left headlight was completely squashed and part of the fender was hanging lose but everyone was okay. The right headlight was also bumped out of alignment in the accident and now somehow the light skewed to the right, leaving the left side of the road in complete darkness, while the road edge and bush on the right side of the car was lit up. They drove forward more slowly so as not to hit anything else and get to their destination safely.

The entire road trip was 385 kilometres but with the two small girls, Tess and Anna and the girl's mother, Merrin, in the car, they made more stops than the local garbage truck.

Harry and Ken had had a tip off from a mate that they could make a lot of money working the summer on a wheat and sheep farm. Joe, the farmer needed some help with the harvest for the summer on his extensive property. Anna was four years old and she was awake. She stood up on the back seat and leaned over the front seat, looking out the front window between her father and her uncle. Her head bumped onto the ceiling whenever they hit a bump in the road. At four years of age she enjoyed the car seat's suspension as if it were a trampoline at the local fair.

'What's that on the road Dad?' There was a thud on the side of the car.

'Jesus! That was a snake mate, a bloody big snake,' Ken said. 'I said it *was* a snake because he's a dead snake now. And it sounded like he flipped up and hit the side of the car.' laughing loudly at his own joke.

'I'm scared!'

'No need to be scared darling, he's dead.' Ken said lifting her onto his lap in the front seat. The car pulled to a halt in front of the main homestead—a large corrugated iron barn sat nestled in between two huge eucalyptus trees to the right of the home and in the distance. Another sizeable house was set further back behind the main homestead. Each house had its own shading trees and a small patch of manicured green grass at the front.

Anna jumped out of the car first and Merrin followed her. The property looked beautiful in the orange and purple hues of the setting sun.

'What are you doing?' Merrin asked, as she spotted Anna walking on the tips of her toes through the brown dust.

'I'm trying not to step on any of those snake things!' Anna said with a nervous giggle.

Joe greeted them when their car pulled up in front of the farmhouse. Tess was asleep in the backseat of the car huddled in amongst pillows and blankets. Harry carried Tess, and Joe showed them to the guesthouse. Inside, this big old rambling country home felt bigger with high ceilings, a family room with fireplace and a long hallway with lots of bedrooms. Each bedroom had a door outside to a wide veranda that wrapped around the entire building. They had the place all to themselves.

Harry and Ken found a few beers and a good spot on the veranda to rest up and commemorate the drive. They had a makeshift dinner of toasted sandwiches and sat together for a while on the veranda to watch the stars.

'I'm so tired Harry, I'm off to sleep. Good night,' Merrin said, taking the girls with her and leaving them to go to bed.

The two brothers drank into the early hours of the morning, and they managed to be up at first light to go off to work with Joe. It was hot and dusty work and a temperature of 40 degrees made the work especially difficult. Harry and Ken were city boys. Joe went easy on them on their first day, so they finished around three in the afternoon.

They arrived at the house just in time for afternoon tea in an old Ute and a cloud of dust. They looked drained and dirty, and went straight for the beers in the fridge.

'Girls, Joe says the fair is in town. We should go into town after dinner!'

'Really! Can we Dad?' said Anna, jumping up and down.

'Yep, go get dressed up and tell your mother,' Harry said, knocking the lid off another bottle.

When Anna and Tess came out of the house a little while later, they were dressed for the fair and Anna was still jumping up and down like a wallaby.

'We're going to the fair, we're going to the fair!'

'There'll be fireworks and fairy floss,' Ken said from the steps.

Neither Harry, nor Ken had showered and they continued to sit around drinking and smoking, filthy, covered in dust and sweat from head to toe.

'Get us some dinner first love, and then we'll get cleaned up.'

Dinner was a long drawn out affair. Talk got louder and the behaviour more rowdy; the beers kept on coming, as it got later and later.

'Let's go Dad!' Anna said excitedly, cutting into the conversation. 'Let's go to the fair.'

'Don't be rude, your uncle was speaking.' Harry said, in an icy tone, 'We'll go when I say.'

'You said we could go.' Anna pleaded.

'Now we're not going at all.' He snapped at her suddenly.

Anna bit down on her lip and tears welled in her eyes. Her uncle pulled her towards him and squeezing her too tightly; he leaned over and kissed her on the cheek. His kiss was wet and sloppy with alcohol and smoke. Anna made a face and pulled away from him.

'Come on girls,' Merrin said, sounding too cheerful, 'Let's go inside away from the mosquitoes and I'll read you a story.'

Drinks were followed with more drinks. Harry spotted a whip hanging on a hook on the veranda. He moved to take it down and kicked over the empty glass bottles as he stepped forward.

'Sshhhit! You'll wake the girls,' he laughed drunkenly, picking up the whip. It was beautifully made, intricate strips of fine leather plaited together, wide at the handle end, gradually getting finer, down to the finest tip at the other end and finished off with a tailpiece—one thin strip of leather.

'Don't wake the babies,' he said again, as he wobbled a little down the stairs, and then straightened himself up standing with his feet shoulder width apart, taking a moment to stabilize himself. He raised his arm and brought the whip down fast, flicking it high into the air. It made a loud swishing sound as it came past his ears.

'This is great, I can do this—Ken watch this!' flicking the whip again.

'Crack,' went the whip, sounding like a gunshot.

'Give me a turn smart arse,' Ken said, jumping up out of his seat.

'No,' wait.

'Crack,' went the whip echoing into the night. 'Good one, give me a try,' Ken said, ripping the whip out of Harry's hands. Ken had a smoke hanging out of the right side of his mouth. Smoke was going into his eyes, as he raised the whip awkwardly at an angle, and brought it down hard. It swished through the air, whipping the cigarette out of his mouth and sending its red ember flying.

'Fuck,' yelled Ken holding his face.

Harry was laughing when Ken came back to get his beer. The light from the lamp shone on his face, where Harry could see the welt raised high on Ken's face. It left a trail from his forehead to his mouth, over his right eye.

'That's gotta hurt like a bitch!' said Harry, nearly falling off his chair laughing.

In the morning when Anna and Tess came to the breakfast table, no adults were up yet—it seemed—so they had some cornflakes with milk and went outside to play.

There were beer bottles strewn all over the veranda. Cigarette butts scattered over the sparse grass at the foot of the stairs. The girls stood on the veranda and surveyed the mess.

As they looked across the lawn they spotted a small paddling pool by the fence, under the shade of the jacaranda tree. The pool was empty when they got there but right beside it was a water tap with a bright green hose attached. Tess picked up the hose and turned the tap on to let the water run in.

'You shouldn't get so excited all the time, Anna,' Tess said, leaning over and placing her arm around Anna's shoulders.

'What do you mean?'

'You get so excited about fairs and things and then they never happen!'

'I can't help it!' Anna said, exasperated.

'If you stop getting excited—you won't get so upset.' she added, turning the tap on and aiming it into the pool.

'I like getting excited about things,' Anna said, shaking her sisters hug off, 'We just didn't go to the fair this time.' She took her pyjama pants off and then in just her underpants, sat in the pool and watched the water rise. 'Maybe we can go another day?' she added placing a purple jacaranda flower in the slipstream of the hose and watching it float away.

The two sisters splashed each other playfully; they lay on their stomachs and pretended to swim as the water level rose further. Tess stepped out of the pool and grabbed the hose again. She turned the water pressure up and pointed the hose towards Anna in the pool.

'Swim under the tunnel,' she squealed to Anna as she made the water arch and delighted in making swirling patterns with the hose.

Anna swam under the arched water. Suddenly, she noticed a big brown snake appear from under the house in the distance and make its way across the lawn towards her. She pointed at the snake coming directly towards them. She opened her mouth to speak but no words came out. Tess was distracted playing with the hose swirling it all around and singing.

'Snake!' She finally managed in a screeching voice. As Tess turned around, Joe the farmer was there in a flash. He had a hoe in his hand and he bought it down hard on the head of the snake, right in front of the girls. He cut off its head and the body writhed and wrapped itself up around the handle, writhing and wriggling and twirling around the wood. Tess and Anna just sat there watching, with mouths wide open—gaping.

Lunch was served in the farmhouse with lots of food and lively conversation. Anna wasn't hungry, her skin felt itchy and she was hot.

'I don't feel good mum, my neck hurts,' said Anna, as she hopped off her chair and walked over to Merrin.

'Open your mouth, poke your tongue out and go aaarh!' Merrin instructed her daughter. 'Your tonsils are red raw!'

'She has a temperature too,' Merrin said to Harry sitting at the table.

'Mum, what's that?' Anna asked as she noticed movement under the table.

'Oh my God,' Merrin screamed.

'Look Mum, another snake under the table.'

'Oh my godfather,' Merrin screamed again, jumping up onto her chair and pulling Anna up with her.

Harry put the cake cover over the snake to contain it and Joe picked the striped snake up with one hand and the cake cover with the other.

'Quick thinking Harry,' he said, with a big smile on his face.

'This one's nothing to worry about.'

'How can you tell?'

'You really have to know your snakes. This is just a python, he won't hurt anyone.'

'It's the drought bringing them. They are looking for a drink of water,' Harry said.

'Just keep the screen doors shut and that will keep them out.' Joe said.

The girls went to their room to have a rest; four single bunk beds all in a line—

'Girls, you can't leave the doors open—you heard what Joe said, the snakes will come in.'

'I want to go home, I hate it here!' Tess said, beginning to cry.

Anna snuggled under her blankets, pulling them around her and tucking them in tight. Shivering she tried to close her eyes and go to sleep.

'Mum, I'm itchy, I want to scratch my whole body off, I'm so itchy,' Tess said laying on her bed and scratching her stomach,

'Let me have a look at you—you have little blisters on your stomach. I don't know what they are. Let me go and get your father.'

'Looks like chicken pox!' said Harry with a beer in his hand.

'Tonsillitis *and* chicken pox! Are we having a good holiday yet girls?'

Psychodrama

Her legs were longer when she looked at them from this angle, disproportionate to the rest of her body and it hurt to try and touch her toes.

'How long did it take you to do that?' Anna asked the very flexible woman beside her on a pink yoga mat.'

'It doesn't take long when you persevere!' she replied softly.

'But it's so painful.'

'You stay with the body and talk gently to it, by breathing into the muscles and it will go where you want it to, eventually.'

'Does getting more control over your body help you gain more control in your life?'

'Definitely, I think so.'

'Does getting more control over your mind help as well?'

'Yes, if you are interested we're all going along to a psychodrama class tonight.

'Sure, I'd love to come along.'

Anna arrived at the surf club for an introductory session in psychodrama in the early evening. The sun was setting on the horizon and an orange sky reflected brightly on the dark rippled ocean. The people were friendly, everyone seemed to be happy and involved and they supplied pizza, great pizza! They didn't explain anything about the process but talked mainly about energy and getting energy flowing in the body. They did some group exercises together, then some dancing, and by the end of the evening Anna decided to go on their five-day retreat. She had made a friend called Carla, who told her that the venue was in the hills, only a few hours drive away and she offered that they travel there together, in Carla's vehicle.

Anna and Carla arrived late in the afternoon. They got a little lost; missing a turnoff and driving fifty kilometres in the wrong direction. Anna had been so engrossed in the conversation she hadn't been watching the map.

'Oh well, it's such a beautiful day for a drive. Isn't this countryside gorgeous?'

'God—whenever I was with Joe and we got lost, he'd lose it.'

'Why?'

'I don't know, he'd just lose his shit and get all angry and stuff and always blame me.'

'That's ridiculous,' said Carla laughing. 'Getting lost is part of the journey.'

'Actually, Shane was like it as well.' Anna sighed deeply. 'I feel like I've been lost and hanging out with angry people most of my life,' Anna said smiling to herself.

'We're all lost to some degree—that's what makes life interesting. My ex would lose it over money!'

Carla pulled over at a petrol station. They bought petrol, a few ice creams and sat and enjoyed the country air and the fact that they were both free to get lost.

They arrived just as the sun was setting and met the others. Twenty-eight people had gathered to play together for five days of psychodrama. Anna didn't even fully understand what psychodrama was; she just knew that she wanted to make changes to herself by doing something different than what she had been doing, and this was different.

Fifteen cabins scattered on the property around the main building that housed the seminar room, which was large and spacious. There was a mess hall that was more like a country kitchen and a large dining room off to the side with tables and chairs that easily seated fifty people, so there was room to move about and choose dining conversation. Large fireplaces in each room made the main room, the dining room and the kitchen warm and inviting in the cold winter weather.

Carla and Anna found a vacant little cabin, back from the others. It was the same size and design as all of the other cabins: basic and cost effective, with wooden walls, wooden floorboards and a corrugated iron roof. None of the cabins had heating inside, only a fire—place outside, which consisted of a circle of rocks around a shallow hole in the dirt and a pile of wood stacked nearby.

Some people were four to a cabin. Carla and Anna claimed their cabin and no others came, so they had the extra space for themselves. Carla took the top bunk on the left side of the cabin and Anna took a single bunk on the right side.
About fifty-metres away, in the centre of the cabins, was a shower block with toilets and three showers.

Everyone gathered together in the mess hall for dinner at seven o'clock. After dinner all of the participants, twenty women and eight men, gathered together for orientation. Everyone was seated in a circle. Karl stood up and stepped forward to introduce himself.
'Welcome everyone, tonight we will be doing introductions and begin our work together tomorrow. I want your stay here to be comfortable, so get a good night's sleep tonight,' Karl said with a big smile. Karl was a psychotherapist. He was American.
'I've trained all over the world in psychodrama,' he told everyone. 'I've done groups in France and Mexico, Italy and Spain.'

He was tall and cocky, with blue eyes and a smile that spread across his face like a pearl necklace. His white sports shirt had a navy trim that matched his track pants. His runners were white and bright, straight out of the box.

A middle-aged man, called Kim, whispered something to the woman sitting next to him.

'If you have something to say Kim, let the whole group hear it.'

'I was talking to my wife, Karl!'

'Well you were talking while I was talking Kim—so I think the whole group might be interested in what you have to say.'

'Well if you must know, I don't want to be here. And I correct myself, my ex-wife! I am only here because she won't let me see my son if I don't change. But I don't want to be here because I have no issues.'

'It sounds like you have something going on, Kim.'

'I told you I don't want to be here.'

'No one is making you stay here. You have free choice. Know that you can leave now, tonight before the work begins.'

'This is all very awkward!' Anna thought to herself sitting directly across from him. There was a long silence and then Kim stormed off in a huff, slamming the door behind him.

'See you all bright and early in the morning at 7am sharp!' Karl said abruptly, clapping his hands together and standing up to leave the room.

The group broke up, some went straight to their cabins to sleep, others went to the bathroom and the rest stayed talking around the fire, drinking coffee and teas and thinking about what tomorrow would bring.

Anna walked to her cabin. It was dark and the lack of streetlights made the stars stand out more, like a quilt of glitter overhead. She took no time at all falling off to sleep and she slept well except for waking up once during the night extremely hungry, and satisfying her hunger with a banana.

First thing in the morning she took a short walk along the narrow path, through tall eucalyptus, melaleuca and balga grass trees to the showers. Anna felt happy to breathe in the fresh air. After a shower and a beautiful country breakfast the group gathered in the main room around the fireplace.

'You want to be present in your mind and in your body today!' Karl spoke with a serious tone. 'The best way to do this is to be grounded.'

He grabbed one of the assistants—a blonde haired, attractive woman called Tracey and held hands with her, leaning backward and away from her grip.

'Bend your knees, breathe, and take the weight into your ankles. Pull the energy from the earth up into your body and push the energy from your body down into the earth!'

'Find a partner.' Karl yelled, letting Tracey move onto someone else.

'This is so important!—Bend your knees with your legs slightly parted. It sounds easy but it isn't—we're going to hold it for five minutes!' Karl instructed taking a seat on the stool near the fire.

Anna held hands with Carla and leaned back and out away from her. Her legs didn't like the position even for one minute and she felt shooting pains going up into her thighs.

'Bend you knees and squat a little, you know that you are doing it right when you can feel it in your legs.' Carl explained further, smiling at the girls nearest to him.

The grounding process actually scared Anna. You had to bend your knees and squat down, bringing the energy up from the ground, into your body through your feet. For some reason Anna found this extremely painful.

'Urrgh! This kills, my legs are shaking and I can't believe how painful it is.'

'Stay with it—it will help your process,' said Carla.

'You need to do at least ten minutes of that and when you have finished with that—rotate onto the rollers. Rolling your spine will open up all of the energy centres in your body. Choose a colour—start rolling.'

The rollers were provided in a variety of colours—Each roller was made of thick industrial black plastic tubing sixty centre metres wide and forty high. The colour of each roller matched the colour of the energy centres in the body. The colour red resonated with the base chakra, orange for the sexual centre, yellow for the solar plexus, green for the heart chakra, blue for the throat, violet for the third eye. Anna chose a red roller and began rolling her back. She liked the feeling of stretching out her spine. Others chose to jump up and down on brightly coloured exercise balls. Anna thought they looked like big kids playing in kindergarten. They straddled the ball with a leg on either side and sat on it holding onto the handles between their legs. These coloured balls some how took their weight and they bounced happily around the room.

Mid morning, after all of the physical exercise, the mood changed. Karl called everyone into a circle and then 'The Process' began. One at a time a person went into the centre of the circle created by the twenty-eight participants. Karl facilitated 'The Process,' and he chose who would go into the centre of the circle to work on their issue. Kim was chosen first. Anna was surprised he hadn't left from the way he had spoken to Karl the night before. Yet here he was talking about his mother and how much she had humiliated him. Now he wanted a female from the group to volunteer, so that he could act out revenge of that humiliation on her.

'Oh no!' Anna said, stepping backwards and suddenly feeling sick to her stomach.

At that moment she knew somehow that she had been deeply humiliated, and she knew that he was going to pick her.

She knew it in her bones that he was going to pick her. Suddenly, without talking to anyone, she knew that the feeling of deep humiliation was in her body.

'He's going to pick you,' Carla said coming quickly towards her.

'I know.'

'That's great.'

'What's great about it?'

'He's going to shift humiliation.'

'Apparently I have loads of that.'

'That's great—you get to get in touch with that and you'll shift it too!'

'Maybe I don't want to get in touch with that!'

'You do, you really do.'

'I don't! Trust me. I really don't. I just don't know how I haven't noticed this before?'

'Volunteer, he's going to pick you.'

'I know he's going to pick me. Why do you think I'm hiding back here?'

'It's just pretending, you won't get hurt!'

'What do you mean, I won't get hurt?'

Kim pushed through the group—he seemed to looking for someone in particular. He spotted Anna and pointed straight at her.

'I choose her!'

Everyone seemed excited at his choice. Anna felt really sick now, looking around for the exits.

'It will be fine,' an older woman said to her, patting her on the shoulder.

People scattered around grabbing bits of foam and building a solid shape with it.

'Anna, are you willing to support Kim in his process?' Karl asked.

'Well that depends, what's involved?'

'Either you are willing to support him to heal or you are not!' said Karl seriously.

The group assured Anna that they would protect her with pillows and bolsters.

'It's only acting,' an older man called Paul said smiling.

'I want to fuck my mother up the arse until she's dead!' announced Kim proudly. 'And I want her to be my mother,' he said pointing at Anna. Anna was shocked; she was speechless. 'How could things deteriorated so quickly?' She thought to herself.

'Really,' she said out loud surprising herself and trying not to embarrass herself.

'Is this a common practice, people wanting to fuck their mother up the arse until she's dead?' she whispered under her breath to Carla.

'I've never heard of this before, but you just have to go with whatever comes up.'

'Why did this have to come up with *ME*?' Anna whispered to Carla again. Carla laughed and gave Anna a big smile.

'It's really no big deal. Just lie down and imagine something else and let him do his thing—you don't have to do anything—just lay there and we'll look after you.'

How could Kim want to fuck his mother up the arse? Like really, how could he?' Anna thought.

'It's not for us to judge—it's just whatever he needs to do for his healing.'

Anna allowed herself to be to led to the foam props, where she was asked to lay down, and all of the people busied themselves in covering her with more foam pillows while she lay there feeling embarrassed and ashamed. Shame filled her body and she felt sick.

'You are a prop in this scenario—helping this man express his rage at his mother.' Karl explained. 'Take that, you stupid bitch!' Kim yelled his rage out of his body; he thrust his pelvis at the foam and at Anna's body beneath the foam.

'Die you fucking bitch. Die!'

Throughout the whole process, which only lasted a few minutes, Anna watched, amazed that somehow she was the other half of this scene. Kim acted out fucking his mother until she was dead. Anna acted out his mother well. She wasn't really doing any acting; she was just lying there watching. When he finished, Anna closed her eyes and pretended to be dead and Kim fell back on the pillows and was spent.

After a few more processes the group broke up for lunch. Anna left the building. On the way back to her cabin, she passed Kim's cabin. He was sitting on the veranda with his guitar. He invited her to sit with him and he played. Tears rolled down Anna's cheeks, she didn't know why she was crying. He went and got a journal and shared a few poems he'd written. Anna felt kind of comfortable with Kim, and that made no sense to her whatsoever.

All afternoon the processes continued, some moved Anna deeply. The most amazing things in other people's processes moved her. Tears rolled down Anna's cheeks often during the day. She marvelled at *the human being:* in pain, in loneliness, in grief, and in emotional action. It all touched her heart. In each process, these strangers acted out their life pain and in their acting Anna watched and learned and saw reflections of aspects of herself and her own family.

The evening meal was served at seven thirty. Anna was physically and emotionally exhausted. She knew that she should eat, but somehow wasn't hungry. On the way out of the kitchen she grabbed some bananas, in case she got hungry later, and headed off to bed.
Anna tossed and turned and could not get to sleep—the day's events were swimming in her mind. Finally, around midnight, she was hungry, so she reached over in the dark to get a banana without waking Carla up.

'What are you doing?' asked Carla in a sleepy voice.

Anna's mouth was so stuffed full of banana that she garbled an answer through the delicious yellow mush in her mouth.

'I can't sleep,' Anna said.

'You'll need your rest, this is just the first day and you'll be doing it all again tomorrow.'

'You people are seriously messed up!'

'Why?'

'This stuff is twisted! Especially my little acting debut this morning.'

'Yes that certainly was an intense way to begin psychodrama!'

'Why didn't you tell me that kind of thing could happen?'

'I have never seen that before, it's just whatever comes up for people!'

'Who would have thought something so disturbing could come up, and involve me?'

'Like I said before—I know it was an intense way to start the retreat, but look at it this way—it can only get better—and what are the chances of anything like that happening again?'

'When I heard Kim speak on the first night, I thought he was a proper dick head. And then I was surprised he was here this morning, he was doing so much complaining last night.'

'Yeah! Think about his poor wife.'

'Ex wife!'

'Oh yes.'

'But afterwards—like after he fucked me up the arse until I was dead, I thought he'd never talk to me again, but he did—we sat in the sun and he played his guitar and read me poetry and he's a really lovely guy.'

Anna listened in the silence to her words echoing in the cabin around her, and how wrong they were, and then she laughed. She and Carla laughed so much that their faces ached as much as their stomachs.

'Yes, such a lovely guy,' Anna sighed. The cabin was filled with an energy that was so intense, so alive and happy.

Anna felt the weight of human suffering lift off each participant as they played out their story in front of her and the whole group. Each process felt like a sacred event. Each person's process was a piece of intimate theatre. Every process, a confrontation of the unconscious, acted out consciously, exposed in the light, in the arena. Anna had never been with such courageous people before. The audience was respectful to each actor. When the time came for the next participant—Karl decided who would be next in the centre of the circle. Each time the centre of the circle awakened, with something that was so electric, you could almost touch it. Anna was transfixed with each unfolding. And the days passed.

Each night Anna craved bananas. Carla stopped asking her what she was doing—and if she did, it would just set the two of them off laughing again. Her body ached from all of the grounding and the rolling and the dancing workouts before the process began. Whenever a woman did the grounding process they would be supported by another woman and usually men would do the process in pairs.

Anna knew that her time was approaching. Karl asked each participant to write him a letter, stating what they wanted out of the process. In her letter to Karl, Anna expressed her fears. 'I always feel so frail, like a fractured piece of glass. I want to feel strong and in control of myself,' she wrote.

On the fourth day, Anna woke at 5am. She did her meditation and went for a long walk with Carla. They gathered their towels and toothbrushes and headed to the showers. Only one of the three showers in the block, had hot water. Anna looked up at Carla with a twinkle in her eye.

'I'm having the hot water,' she joked, sprinting up the pathway laughing.

'Not if I get there first,' Carla responded racing beside her. The two women raced towards the shower block and laughed like little kids.

Anna laughed in the shower; she'd won the race, the hot water washing away the sweat from the long walk and the race. She felt alive and happy—happier than she had for a very long time.

'Here they are, the naughty kids who woke the whole camp,' announced Karl in a playful voice, when they entered the mess hall for breakfast, still laughing.

After lunch Anna challenged Karl by sitting in the hot seat.
'I'm ready to have my turn.'
'No. It's not your turn, but when it is, it will be amazing,' Karl answered earnestly.
Anna returned to her seat feeling disappointed. She felt so ready, so in her heart, she thought, and then, as she was sitting quietly out of the very back of her mind came a voice, with such clarity and such intensity, that it shocked her to her core.
'No fucking man is going to tell *me* when to have my turn.'

A guy called Ned had his time in the circle. Ned had been ruthlessly beaten by his father all of his life, on the family farm. As an adult, Ned had done seven years in prison for manslaughter. This man had so much love in him and so much hurt, and all he wanted, all he ever wanted, was for his father to acknowledge him and love him. The whole group was deeply touched—there was sobbing and snot running everywhere; not a dry eye in the house, as everyone connected to Ned's pain.

It was the fifth and final day of the retreat and everyone had made connections with people. Anna felt close to many, and she had enjoyed everyone except one guy called Larry. He seemed very popular with all of the other women. Anna had not ever made eye contact with him the entire time, nor did she want to—she didn't like him one bit.

Lunchtime, on this last day, came and Anna was feeling pretty bad. Her neck was so stiff and tight that she was in agony. It was as if the muscles in her neck were being squeezed in a vice. She felt trapped and frightened. She wanted to go to the toilet, she wanted to vomit, but she couldn't. She had her period. She had haemorrhoids. She felt toxic.

'What the hell is going on?' she thought to herself. This had never happened before. She felt so nauseous that she couldn't eat anything. She took a walk in the bush. When she was a few hundred yards away from the main house she felt sick again. She tried to vomit.

'I'm hurting, I'm hurting!' rang out in her head and in her body. She saw her reflection in the window of her cabin, her brow wrinkled. She looked old and grey, like the colour of the sky. Grey, as if a poison were flowing through her veins, eating away at her. She couldn't be sick so she stuck her fingers down her throat. Her head throbbed and throbbed like a fire alarm. She wanted to die. Anna was hurting so much. She knew that she couldn't run now so she gathered all of her strength, and walked back to the main room, dragging her body with her.

The group had already gathered and the session had begun. They were dancing and doing more grounding. Anna knew she was next up. She began to move slowly at first, listening to the music and moving more took the focus off her pain. The more she danced, the better she felt. Amazing herself, she started jumping higher and higher and then doing karate kicks. Even as sick as she was feeling, a part of her felt strong, like a warrior now.

'This is so weird,' Anna said out loud to no one in particular.

The music stopped and everyone gathered in the circle—all but one other woman, had already had their turn in the centre.

'Anna it is your turn now.' Karl talked softly.

Instead of a woman to help her to do the grounding process, Karl picked Paul to assist Anna. He walked towards Anna and held out his hands to hold hers. They faced each other getting ready and then he apologised and said he had to take his jumper off. When he turned around to face Anna, any fear she had of the process subsided, when a huge gorilla looked at her from the front of Paul's T-shirt.

'You're the reason I've been eating all of these bananas.'

'What are you feeling?' Karl asked, after the grounding process.

'Tightness in my stomach and all the way down the front of my body.'

Karl pushed a roller towards her. The roller was covered with fine layers of foam and then enclosed with bright red material.

'Use this, roll on your stomach and massage the front of your body and you will release those feelings,' Karl said calmly, leaning on the wall in front of her and looking over out to the audience.

Anna got down on her hands and knees, putting the weight of her body onto the roller. She massaged her stomach and solar plexus, by rolling her body slowly backwards and forwards. She was surprised at how quickly the angry growling began to rumble deep down in her belly. This sound had substance. It splashed up from her stomach into her chest and throat.

Liquid like the ocean, potent like poison, her deep hatred lay smirking in the blackness inside her. Anna tried to pretend that nothing was happening at first, but then she sat back squatting, her arms resting on the roller in front of her, taking in the audience, as if she was pleased that so many people had showed up to meet her.

'What's your name?' Karl asked, noticing the change in her.

'I am the Goddess of Hate,' Anna announced with a proud tone, shocking herself.

'How long have you been with Anna?'

'Since she was two.'

'What made you come?'

'That's when he first did it to her.' Tears rolled down Anna's cheeks.

'What's happening?' Karl asked, watching her closely. 'Where are you?'

'I'm in a cot. He's sticking his fingers into me,' she choked, sobbing. She wanted to recoil from what was happening, she wanted to run away, but her body was frozen. Looking up again, she was taken by surprise to see all of the people in the group. They'd been so quiet watching her that she'd forgotten that they were there. She felt a part of her shrivelling under the spotlight, recoiling away from the crowd.

'Come on!' yelled Karl, 'Don't try to tell us that you're shy!' he added, scaring her out of the moment. Anna laughed out loud. She was angry and confident now, changing back again, and the change surprised her as she stood up and strutted over to him, leaning her face towards his.

'That's right, I'm not shy.' She said, surprising herself again with her words. She had, all of her life been very shy, so shy that she could never speak in front of others without blushing bright red and feeling frozen. Anna was impressed with Karl for noticing this other part of her.

Anna faced Karl now with a new confidence.

'I want you to know, that I get it, 'here,' better than you do,' she said, touching her temple to emphasize how much smarter than him she was.

'And I get it 'here,' better than you do!' she said, even louder. Touching her heart and puffing out her chest to show him how much better than him she felt things, and finally she finished with a pelvic thrust in his direction yelling, 'And I get it 'here,' *so* much better than you do!'

Anna knew that she got 'everything,' so much better than he did and she felt *so* much better than him! Walking through the audience, she stopped in front of a man called Ned. In Ned's session the day before the entire group sobbed in empathy with him about his brutal sad life. Anna arched her back in front of Ned, she held her arms outstretched and screamed.

'I have suffffffffffeeeerrrred, more than you have.'

'Good Anna! Now who sexualized you when you were a child?' Karl asked.

'No one,' Anna answered.

'That's not what you said a moment ago. So what's all this about then?'

'This is intense that's what this is!'

'Who was it?'

The group were sitting all around her now, in a large circle, all eyes fixed on her. As if she had eyes in the back of her head and without shifting her gaze from Karl, she pointed behind her to a fair haired, weathered man with pock—marked skin called Larry.

'He did!'

Only after she chose him, did she notice how much he resembled her own uncle. Karl asked Larry to come and stand in front of Anna and to represent her uncle for her. Anna had blocked it out but now the feelings in her body made sense to her.

'Tell him what you think of him,' Karl instructed.

'I hate you!' Anna screamed at the skinny man in front of her.

'Good work,' Karl said, as he handed her a large carved wooden sword. It was heavy in her hands.

The audience had obviously done this before. They worked feverishly to set up the scene. Anna stood alone in the centre of the room with a sword in her hand and tears flowing down her face. They placed a thick block of foam in between herself and her uncle's representative. Karl stood beside Anna and the group formed a circle around them. The foam was waist high. Anna looked into Larry's face and brought the sword down hard on the bolster, screaming at him as she did. Karl showed her how to tilt her hips forward, as she brought the sword down.

'Good work Anna. Each time you hit out and thrust your pelvis forward like that, you are releasing all of that unwanted sexual energy from your body—get it out.'

Anna hit the bolster dozens of times, yelling at him and venting her anger.

'I hate you! You stole my childhood. You took away my trust!'

Anna cried and cried and then something else happened. Each time she raised the sword above her head she began to feel stronger. Suddenly, in her mind, flashed a different scene, a violent sword fight, a battle of Samurai. She felt the blood of this aristocratic caste pump through her veins and she knew that she was *that* warrior. The swords clashed together, the harsh sound of the steel blades crystal-clear in her mind, as she fought off her attackers. She saw blood running down her arms and dripping off her robes as she sliced her foe: beheading them in one single slice and cutting other attackers into pieces. Anna could see herself as *that* fighter. Her black, shiny silk kimono hugged her strong chest and broad shoulders. Her sleeves were folded back and her thick, long black hair was braided into a plait that felt heavy as she flew through the air, slicing her sword with deadly precision.

Anna felt the strength and the atonement in her mind and body that the Samurai felt. She stood alive and triumphant in the battle scene where the bodies of dozens of her attackers lay strewn, decapitated, bloody and dead on the ground around her.

She felt a surge of energy rush into her body and although she could see the people from the healing group standing all around her, supporting her to get free from her grief—in her mind she saw the battle field. She knew that she was a great martial artist—she was a Samurai. Each time she held her arms up, she felt as strong as the steel blade in her hands. Anna felt calm and a sense of balance awaken in her body. Momentarily she was that great warrior, a Samurai who knew how to protect herself and knew how to kill. She knew that she had killed many people. Somehow the strength of the Samurai washed away the fear of the little Anna and in that moment, she stood victorious after a mighty battle. She flicked her long black plaited hair over her shoulder, and slid her beautiful sword back into its sheath that hung from a belt around her waist, exhaled and centred her self.

The energy of shame and hate was replaced with calm, warmth and power. Anna finished. She smiled at the people in the room who had witnessed her experience and she felt a camaraderie and closeness to these people like she had never felt before.

Anna stood in the centre of the circle feeling in awe of herself. She had always felt less than. The pride that she had shown the group was so over the top, and the experience being so much more than everything, and everybody had somehow balanced her, so that now she felt what it might feel to be normal.

She handed the sword back to Karl who was smiling at her warmly.

'Well done!' He said embracing her with a big hug.

'You acted out your pride and you did a brilliant job.'

'Is that what I did?'

'Yes and we are not quite finished.'

'We're not?'

'No.' Karl took her by the hand and led her over to a single mattress on the floor where he gestured for her to lay down.

'Make yourself comfortable. Just lay back and try to relax.'

Karl then spoke to the group as a whole.

'When Anna was two, an entity was allowed to enter her, after the trauma she went through, and now it is time for that entity to leave.'

'What the hell?' Anna went to sit up but Karl put his hand on her shoulder.

'Relax . . . it's going to be alright.'

Some of the men in the group pulled four big white decorated candles to the four corners of the mattress where Anna lay, and lit them. The candles reminded Anna of the ones in her local Church when she was small. Somehow that was comforting to her. One thing that the church and the clergy had expertise in was the celebration of the ceremony. The ceremony created a wonderful atmosphere. Anna was feeling so wonderful and relieved that she did lay back and began to relax. She doubted that she could possibly have an entity—surely one would know if that were the case, she thought to herself.

'People come in closer,' Karl instructed in a very serious manner.

'We thank this energy for being with Anna, for whatever purpose, and now we release it to where it came with love.'

Anna was feeling a little silly for getting all of this attention for something so weird.

'Repeat after me in love and light.' Karl started.

'In the name of Jesus Christ leave Anna now! And keep repeating it together until we see a change.' Karl said.

The whole group chanted this prayer over Anna, as she lay on the pillows feeling comfortable and calm.

'You came to her when she was two years old and I thankyou. It's time to leave her body now.' Karl spoke directly over Anna.

'In the name of Jesus Christ, leave Anna now!' the group continued to chant.

Anna felt a sudden twitch in her left cheek and then a flutter in her stomach. She was breathing deeply, partly because she knew breathing helped everything and partly because now she was feeling nervous.

There was a sudden puffing out in her chest that she didn't feel that she instigated. Both of her cheeks were twitching and she shut her eyes tight. She tried to take her next inhale but instead, something like a gush of wind, left her body through her face and mouth.

Everyone cheered out excitedly as they saw the shift in Anna. A few of Anna's friends came to hug her and Anna stood up and looked around the room feeling different and new.

'If trust had a sound—what would that sound like?' Karl asked the group loudly from the back of the room.

Anna hugged a few people and went to sit on a cushion over by the fireplace.

'Who's up next?' Karl called out eyeing the people in the room. 'Jasmine, you're up.' Jasmine stood in the centre of the circle.

'My mother was crazy when I was little. I think she was insane! I want to deal with that, but I'm frightened,' she opened up to Karl.

'The best thing to do is to face your fear head on,' Karl said. He motioned for one of the women in the group, to lie on the floor.

'Here she is! Your mum's waiting for you—talk to her,' Karl said, flamboyantly.

Jasmine walked around her mother's representative lying on the floor. She put a blanket over her mother's head.

'I don't want to look at you, you stupid bitch!' she yelled. And in the next moment she was lifting the rug up and playing peek-a-boo. Jasmine's antics got more and more ridiculous and Anna started laughing.

'I'm going to grab these and tie them around your head.'

'What is she grabbing?' Anna asked Carla, who was sitting next to her.

'I don't know.'

'There you go you silly bitch, now you're a vagina head,' Jasmine said, sitting back admiring her work.

Anna looked at Carla and they both started laughing. She was outside the circle and she was laughing so hard, her stomach hurt. Rolling backwards on the floor, Anna remembered when she was two years old and everyone thought that her own mother was crazy.

ഗ്ര ഗ്ര ഗ്ര ഗ്ര

Anna remembered going to visit her mother in hospital, in the back of a borrowed utility. Harry picked Tess up and popped her on the top of a spare tyre. He put Anna next to Tess.

'Hold on,' he said brightly, in a voice that sounded as if he was putting them on a merry-go-round at the local fair. Anna tried to hold on the black tarpaulin crumpled in a heap behind the driver's window but she couldn't. So she held onto Tess. The two girls surged forward and then back with the motion of the car until Anna felt sick.

'Jesus Christ,' Harry said loudly from inside the car, as he pulled the car over to the side of the road. He plonked Anna onto the thick grass on the verge. She vomited again. An elderly lady came from a nearby house. Anna remembered the kindness in her voice, kikuyu grass prickling her legs as she sat

down on the side of the road and the noise of white sheets being ripped into rags to clean her up.

By the time they made it to the hospital, visiting hours were over.

'See what you've done now! You're enough to send anyone crazy! Wait here,' Harry said.

Anna watched the pretty lead light glass in the entrance door, twinkle in the fading sunlight. Harry pushed through the doorway and disappeared into the building.

Chelmsford Gardens were full of flowers. Tall gum trees shaded the gardens from the harsh summer sun. The sky-blue utility sat still now on the bitumen driveway. Bellbirds called out to each other echoing in the landscape.

While Harry was gone, Tess and Anna played 'I spy,' with the passenger door open and Anna sat on the ground outside the car.

'I spy with my little eye, something beginning with D,' said Anna.

'Door,' offered Tess.

'No.'

'Driveway.'

'No.'

'Doctor,' said Tess, noticing a man with a white coat tripping out the front door of the hospital. The Doctor was waving his arms in the air and yelling, 'You can't do this!' after Harry pushed him over.

Harry walked away, towards the car, cradling something in his arms. Anna noticed how his head tilted to the side when he was serious. He had a way of holding his shoulders when he walked that reminded Anna of John Wayne, out of the cowboy movies she watched on the television every Saturday afternoon.

'You'll have to get into the back again girls,' he said.

'Who's that?' Anna asked, looking at the emaciated partially dressed figure her father placed on the front seat. Tattered white hair fell over the pale face and her eyes were closed.

'That's Mummy.'

'What happened to her arms?' asked Anna, in a raised voice looking at the deep purple bruises around her mother's wrists.

'Don't you worry, honey,' said Harry, lighting a cigarette.

He tucked the blanket around her. 'She'll get better at home with us. I have my beautiful girl back. She's my living doll, and we're going home!'

'She's not a doll Daddy!' *Anna said, to correct him.*

'Yes she is darlin, she's Daddy's living doll.'

Grandfather

Ronald was tall with dark hair and dark rings under his eyes. He lived quietly, in a little wooden cottage in the inner city. He didn't sleep well, and he read books way into the early hours of the morning. He loved to write and he was good at it because he had lived a full life with many experiences to draw upon. He wrote political speeches. He was passionate and full of thoughts and dreams of how life should be. Other people spoke his words because he was shy and he didn't like to be in the limelight.

As a child and young boy he loved exploring. When he wasn't riding his beloved horse, he was running on his long cross-country runs. He was now slim and wiry. Despite his age, there was still a strength showing subtly, from under his tired skin. Once, long ago, he was energetic and athletic.

Ronald had fallen in love young, and got married. The marriage turned sour quickly when kids came along more rapidly than the money to feed them. The woman he married was Irish and her name was Mara Murphy. She lost her temper often. She liked to throw saucepans at him and the walls to express her rage. When news came of war, he was glad to go, to get away from her. She was as hard as hate. He left his home and travelled abroad by ship. He got to take his horse with him.

He survived the war. He wished he hadn't. He wandered the world until he grew weary of it. When he came home he just wanted peace, so he didn't look up his wife, Mara. He couldn't face the violence in her and that was all he could remember about her. He knew it was wrong, but maybe it was better this way. He lost his horse. He had to shoot her before he came home from the Middle East. He'd lost his big brother and most of his friends there too. Ronald had seen too much black. He lived by himself and the blackness engulfed him. He didn't know exactly when it happened but he knew that he was numb.

For years, one day merged with another and nothing had any meaning. Then one day he met one of his sons, grown into a man. Ronald thought that life was looking up and then, even better, she came along. She had a sparkle and laughter in her eyes and without meaning to, she lit up his world. He called her his little sweetheart, his little princess, although her name was Anna, and from the moment she first came to visit they were inseparable. He'd say, 'It's just you and me sweetheart.'

He was wise and kind to her and at night when she slept, it was comforting for her to hear the tap tapping of his typewriter. Although sex wasn't on her mind, she did have strong feelings for him. She liked the feelings that came with his fingers inside her. She liked it when he held her close and loved her. She liked it when, just for a little while he stopped being sad.

Their relationship developed over time. One day while out walking together hand in hand, they bumped into his ex, Mara. She had moved into the area, into the same street. After all of this time, Ronald knew he would bump into her some day. Within a few sentences Mara was yelling at him and they were into an argument about old hurts. Anna felt uncomfortable and embarrassed. Ronald was squeezing her hand too tightly as he finished the conversation and pulled her away faster than her little legs could keep up.

Ronald felt guilty for leaving Mara to bring up the kids on her own.

'Anna, I want to go and visit Mara every now and then.' He said, when they were far enough away from her.

'No!'

'I know that she's nasty to you, but I have to make it better with her.'

'No. I hate her!'

Anna understood that he felt guilty about the past. But she didn't care and she had strong objections to this. It was one thing to have to be with Ronald but quite another to have to put up with her grandmother as well.

Counselling

Counsellor: Okay Anna, from where you sit here today, if you were to imagine a 'future you,' a you who had solved all of your problems now . . . you'd know when that had changed, wouldn't you?

Anna: Yes I would. I'd have more friendships and more intimacy. I would feel included and a part of something bigger than myself.

Counsellor: Good.

Anna: I feel separate now—it's as if I have a wall around me, an invisible wall that keeps me safe but it keeps me separate too. And then in contrast to that—in relationships, I lose myself, like I dissolve into the other person and somehow disappear.

Counsellor: How does that feel?

Anna: It's horrible really, like I feel alone, not so much lonely but alone. I'm here on this planet all by myself, if you know what I mean. Or whenever I'm in relationship, like I feel trapped and it's as if I lose my sense of freedom.

Counsellor: How would you know when that had changed?

Anna: I'd feel more comfortable and calm. I guess I would feel more open.

Counsellor: What would that 'future you' be doing to create that open, calm comfortable feeling?

Anna: I don't know how I would be different. Wow . . . I feel like crying, just becoming aware of it. I think that I have created a wall of protection to shield me from pain but in the end it only cuts me off from people.

Counsellor: Okay, you are aware that you've created a wall around yourself . . . consider that you have all of the resources you need to create the changes that you want to make. Notice the 'future you' free from this wall . . . ask yourself, what do you have to take away from this 'you' now, to be that 'you' in the future?

Anna: Fear, loads of fear.

Counsellor: When you see, and feel, and sense you in the future, having connection with others in a way that feels good to you . . . how does that feel?

Anna: Dangerous!

Counsellor: Dangerous is an interesting adjective don't you think? When did you decide life was dangerous?

Anna: It was dangerous living with alcoholics.

Counsellor: So what makes that connection with friends and relationships, in the future, dangerous? And how do you take the danger away, so that you can have the connection? What if I were to tell you that the way things occur to you isn't real, it's just a bunch of thoughts that you have in your head already about how things used to be and it's not real now.

Anna: Okay, I think that's true. You know I've never really thought about it that way before, but I think that's all it is and I am expecting it to keep being what it was in my past.

Counsellor: What if 'dangerous' was just how it has occurred to you in the past and there is a possibility that the future does not need to occur as dangerously?

Anna: Lots of times I feel overwhelmed and it all feels too hard.

Counsellor: So what are the thoughts running through your mind, that are creating this for you?

Anna: It's too hard, I hate men . . . I'm not good enough, I'm not loveable, relationships are dangerous, I am dangerous. Just a few negative thoughts here and there.

Counsellor: Relationships are dangerous! Can you see and hear those words that you are speaking and feeling and notice how that belief conflicts with wanting to have close relationships?

Anna: Yes, I can see that I learned it while growing up and I expect that to happen again.

Counsellor: How do you want relationships to be?

Anna: I want them to be safe and interesting.

Counsellor: What would it feel like if you had the belief that having close relationships was safe and interesting?

Anna: If relationships occurred to me as safe and interesting and if I was good enough, then I'd be different. I'd be free.

Counsellor: So you would know when that was different, wouldn't you?

Anna: Yes.

Counsellor: Do you put yourself in any situations where you can meet good men?

Anna: Not really. I am often too busy working to go out socially.

Counsellor: I'm hearing you say that in the past relationships have been dangerous and you have made a connection with where these thoughts are coming from and it is the past.

Anna: Yes.

Counsellor: So you can change that for yourself now, by getting clear in what you value most in intimate relationships, for instance safety, kindness, financial independence.

So let us make a list now of some of the most important things that you value about relationships beginning now and continuing forward in your life.

Anna: Safety is important. Love, kindness, and someone who enjoys being graceful in their life; by that I mean does what they love and loves what they do.

Counsellor: Excellent. You have these values of safety, kindness, love, grace, financial security and independence. Now put them in order of their importance to you.

Anna: Safety, love, kindness, fun and financial independence.

Reclaiming Trust

Counsellor: Financial independence for him or for both of you?

Anna: I think that people are responsible for making their own money.

Counsellor: So is safety more important than love and kindness? What do you need to learn from your past relationships so that you can fully and completely be safe and present in relationship?

Anna: As I'm thinking about it now, I think I made some bad choices, and really, if I had love and kindness I would feel safe already.

Counsellor: So now when you know how to recognize and attract love and kindness to yourself—*if trust had a smell, what would trust smell like?*

Fairytale

So this little star lived in the warm glow of a distant sun for what seemed like eternity, waiting and growing impatient, then finally fell to earth. She was confident in herself and her expertise as a great creator. She was so confident, that she chose her parents on purpose because they were worriers—she chose them on purpose because they believed in fear, anger, sickness and sadness. They believed in wishing for nothing so as not to be let down. They believed in hardship because that was what they had learned from their parents and teachers, and their parents and teachers before them.

It surprised her how quickly she forgot, almost everything. Even though she was shiny, bright and full of promise, her parents somehow did not notice. They focused on their problems. So the little star did the best she could—she imagined a secret hatch in her bedroom floor. Each night before she went to sleep she would open the hatch; when no one was watching she would climb down the tunnel that was there down into the earth, going deeper and deeper into the centre.

The earth felt like a mother to her, inviting her deeper inside, deeper beneath the surface. The tunnel was lined with thick intertwined vines. She climbed down the steep hollow by holding onto the vines and lowering herself down. The deeper she climbed, the safer she felt. The deeper she climbed into the earth, the more she remembered. Eventually, she heard the sound of water running and she knew that here, in this special place she was free . . . she loved going deeper into the safety that she needed—inside mother . . . inside earth . . . there she remembered how important it was to mind her mind, no matter what seemed to be happening around her, she needed to mind her thoughts and choose thoughts that nurtured her and nourished her, not just today but yesterday . . . and especially tomorrow.

By day, she lived with her parents who were very unhappy. In her family, more and more, Anna, somehow forgot along the way to stop and smell the flowers, to watch the birds, bees, and insects. Somehow, she forgot to feel the sunshine on her face and breathe the fresh air. Her dreams and aspirations faded. She became full of fear and separate. Moments became less juicy, less jam packed with goodness, and shorter and flatter and somehow squashed so that they went by with a zip. Yes, they went by in a zip, and Anna was really hungry for some fun and for things to make sense to her. Soon each moment had less and less fun, and she was confused. At dinnertime, Anna was forced to eat every skerrick of food on her plate or be severely punished. At school she was forced to learn about a God that punished severely. The longer she stayed with her family, the more she learned about lack; lack of love, lack of money, lack of fun.

Finally, Anna forgot that she was the little star, she turned thirteen and found marijuana. When she had her first joint, she thought that she had found freedom but instead, it was just another negative story. She tried alcohol and that was another dead end. She was tired and desperate and disillusioned with the words . . . Once upon a time . . . and it felt like the end. She didn't want it to be the end, she wanted there to be a tomorrow. In the beginning, she thought tomorrow was going to be excellent. For a long time tomorrow was really, really good but in her mind now, she was at the point of giving up.

ANNA

Early on a Sunday morning Anna and her sister, Tess sat at the beach café. Tess was reading the morning paper and Anna was reading Herman Hesse's *Narcissus and Goldmund*. The breeze was gentle and the sunshine soft on Anna's skin. The café was only half full with people enjoying breakfast.

'You would like this book Tess,' Anna said without looking up from the page.

'What's it all about?' Tess asked, sipping her coffee.

'It's a great story! There are two main characters and they are friends—the first is a monk called Narcissus, he represents science and logic and God and the 'masculine mind'. The other is Goldmund, he wants to be like Narcissus but loves women and being free and traveling; he represents art and nature and the 'feminine mind'. It is so interesting to notice how different they are.' Anna sipped her coffee in the sunshine, watching people walking down to the beach, she travelled back in time daydreaming, and she remembered . . . 'The Annunciation!'

She remembered how she used to say 'The Ann-un-ciation' so rhythmically as a little girl.

'I keep thinking about that word 'Ann-un-ciation,' said Anna playing with the syllables, 'I don't even know what 'the Annunciation' is.'

'It was when Archangel Gabriel came to Mary and told her that she had been chosen by God to have his child—apparently!' Tess told her.

'Really! So, that's that 'immaculate conception,' idea?' Anna asked. 'How does that work?'

'I don't know'

'I mean come on! How does that work?' Anna questioned incredulously, 'It has to be a lark! What a *wild* stretch of the imagination they had . . . in any language, actually in every language. If it was such a magical conception why use a woman? Why didn't he manifest his body out of thin air?'

'Do you remember how much praying we did in our childhood?' Anna asked her sister.

'Yeah, Mum prayed hard every night. It was as if she needed to ward off evil,' Tess said.

'Prayed hard, exactly—it literally felt like hours!'

'We were so little.'

'Hail Mary full of grace, the lord is with thee; blessed art thou among women, and blessed is the fruit of they womb, Jesus.' They recited the prayer in unison.

'Holy Mary, mother of God, pray for us sinners, now and at the hour of our death.' They both burst out laughing.

'Oh my God!'

'We still remember it,' Anna said in disbelief.

'I have not prayed that prayer for a good decade or two.'

'Why am I remembering The Annunciation?' Anna asked herself out loud.

'Because you're crazy—you used to say it a lot—whenever we had to *choose* a decade of the rosary, you chose that one EVERY time. You even got beltings for saying it!'

'What?'

'You must remember getting whacked for saying that.'

'I thought I remembered that and then I thought what a stupid thing to get bashed for and I didn't want to say that out loud—why would I keep saying it?'

'You just kept saying it like you wanted to piss Mum off or something?'

'Maybe I liked the sound of it. It's such a great sounding word. How would I know it was pissing her off when I didn't even know what it meant—I must have been all of five years old.'

'I don't know, it was pretty weird—I just thought you were nuts,' Tess said laughing out loud at her sister.

'Why would I say 'The Ann-un-ciation' to piss her off, when I was five years old?'

'How do I know?'

'Help me understand this—we were kneeling down every night—what else do you remember?'

'We prayed with mum every night—you have no idea how I hated it.'

'I hated it more.'

We each took turns to name a mystery of the rosary—kind of like a special treat and you kept choosing that one again, and again and again.

Anna opened her laptop in the coffee shop and 'googled', 'Rosary.'

'Look! Mum prayed the proper rosary. A rosary has fifty-nine beads: Fifty-three Hail Mary beads, and six Pater Our Father beads. On the circle there are five sets of ten beads separated by four single Pater beads. We went around at least four times: Every night!—the Pope would have been proud.

'Apparently, Pope John Paul II called that rosary the 'Luminous rosary,' Tess joked.

'To me it was the Torturous Rosary and my knees remember every moment,' Anna added.

'I didn't understand why we were praying so much and at school we were taught by the Irish Mercy Sisters so it was all sin and damnation and I didn't want to go to hell.' Tess defended.

'I don't mind the Hail Mary as a prayer—I mean really, except that line which says 'pray for us sinners'—I think that the only sin is fear.' Anna said and pulled a funny face looking at her sister. 'She must have known that we hated it.'

'How long did it go on for!'

'I don't know, it went on for years! I remember the tension in the air—I never knew if you were going to say 'the Annunciation,' again. And then you'd say it again and she'd give you a couple more whacks . . . and the next time she asked—'Who is going to choose a mystery of the rosary tonight?''

'I will,' chirped Anna. 'Really I don't know why I did it. I was so little and I don't remember how much of the church stuff I actually understood—I do remember wanting to mock it.'

'I was so into it. I really believed in her praying and I thought you were so bad or mad,' said Tess.

'You remember it—that's kind of cool. I might think that I was a little crazy if I remembered this stuff all by myself,' said Anna with a serious tone and loving her sister at that moment.

'Mostly I remember there was a long silence, the pause and we waited for your response, thinking surely she's not going to do it again.'

'The Annunciation,' Anna squealed with laughter.

'I can still remember that feather duster sting on the back of my legs and seriously I do not know what possessed me.'

'What made me stop, do you remember?'

'No I don't.'

'Maybe we stopped praying—maybe she just didn't do the rosary thing, we just prayed silently or separately after that.'

'Trust me! I didn't pray after that,' said Anna with relief. 'All of my life I've been aware of the thought that something terrible is going to happen!' she said in a thoughtful voice.

'Life sucks!'

'No it doesn't, it's just beginning to make sense to me, now that I've found out about all of this stuff in my childhood. I made decisions and judgments that I didn't realize would keep on affecting me.'

'I know that's why I said life sucks!'

'But don't you get it, I was right. Something terrible *was* going to happen—it has *already* happened and it doesn't ever have to happen again—I am free of it now, simply by being aware of it!'

'Cool, and also because of the fact that you're a grown up now.'

'Yes, but I could be grown up and not be aware and still stuck. Tess do you understand?'

'Not really.'

'If the truth is that thought is creative, it makes sense to me that I hated men—in the past, not now, but deep in my mind those hateful thoughts were being magnified, and somehow, I projected that stuff onto my partners.'

'So?'

'I'm awake now. That means that I know my conscious mind and my unconscious mind. I have explored my most unreasonable, my most outrageously negative, hateful thoughts from my past, my childhood, my babyhood, and know my weakest innermost thinking. Now that I know that—it makes perfect sense for me to have hated those men in my past.

I have shown myself the life that those shitty thoughts create and it was pretty terrifying shit—especially some of it, I was lucky to survive.'

'Do you really mean to tell me that you take responsibility for all of that?' asked Tess incredulously.

'Yes I want to! Otherwise I give my power away. And besides now it makes sense to me, there are lots of good men out there—I just didn't see them through my negative thoughts and feelings. And that sets me free from those past thoughts and experiences.'

'But—If you have been creating all of these shitty experiences for yourself—what the hell has God been doing?'

'Ha good question!—For me, God is creation; the energy of creation and it gets behind whatever thoughts I have, as if they are real. The question is what is real? And now—in light of my experience with the knowledge that some men creep about at night doing all manner of nastiness—the Annunciation takes on a whole new light. Think about it. Mary—a young girl over two thousand years ago.' Anna stopped talking and took another sip of her coffee.

'Do you think she made it up?' Tess asked nearly choking on her drink.

'How is this any less plausible than the idea of an immaculate conception?' Anna asked incredulously.

'So she gets pregnant and she's surrounded by religious nuts who would not take kindly to her being in the family way—she could have been stoned to death.'

'Yeah—What if she outdid them at their own game and got creative with her own story telling.'

'But the story backfired.'

'How?'

'God became a bloke!'

'Yeah that's true.'

'That's ridiculous.'

'I think God has to be both—masculine and feminine energy.'

'It made me think that I was separate from God . . . I know I hated some particular men, and with good reason and unfortunately that decision included God, if God was masculine and he didn't beam me up out of my situation.'

'Yeah, where was the support?' scoffed Tess.

'When I consider the concept of a feminine aspect of God—I feel excited at the possibilities—wow, if God is feminine maybe I can forgive everything and let it go.' Anna pondered the idea of a Goddess loving and non-judgemental, a God that listened and energised all of her dreams and wishes.

'Makes me feel like I am connected.' She said leaning back, breathing in the salty air and taking in the sunshine.

GESTALT

Therapist: What are we going to work on today?
Anna: I know I was sexually abused when I was little. I suppose I want to talk about it and not feel crazy. I want to make better choices in men . . .

Therapist: What do you mean by feeling crazy and making better choices?

Anna: It makes me crazy that no one wants to talk about sexual abuse.

Therapist: Can you talk to your family?

Anna: You've got to be kidding.

Therapist: What happens?

Anna: I think I have always tried to talk about it, so they consider me 'dangerous,'—you know what will the neighbours think, kind of thing. Like I care what the neighbours think, and let me tell you . . . if it was happening at my house, this stuff was happening at the neighbours' house too. So it's like amnesia happens. It feels like they put cotton wool around themselves. It makes the atmosphere numb and words dissolve in a void.

Therapist: So you've tried to talk about it and they consider that dangerous . . .

Anna: Yes, and I feel that because I wasn't allowed to talk about it—I forgot about it or it went unconscious or something and I was unable to resolve anything. Then I choose abusive men so that I get to experience more of the same shit. It goes around and around and I want to get off this ride.

Therapist: Is there anything else?

Anna: Yes, because I wanted to talk about it—my family feel very uncomfortable around me—they feel that I am dangerous—I have come to think of myself as dangerous and I know that I am not dangerous—I just like to talk about things . . . I also like to imagine things being better—safe and happy and fuller . . . the people in my family don't want to imagine anything at all . . . it's all the same, just about surviving, and they treat me badly.

Therapist: Let's work on that then shall we?

Anna: How will we do that?

Therapist: It's called Gestalt—and it's a bit like play-acting. I want you to come over here on the couch. *(Therapist gives Anna a small doll and gestures towards the couch)* This doll represents childhood. I want you to lay back here and relax and hold this doll. I want you to go back to the first time that you were abused. Know that you are safe and you can just let yourself go.

Anna lay back just as the therapist had instructed and as she was relaxing she started having memories within a few minutes.

Therapist: What is happening?

Anna: He's coming into the room, he's coming over to my cot, he's touching me. He is touching me!

Therapist: Okay. So now step away from that place and where would your mother be if she was in the room right now?

Anna: She would be over there, as if she was outside the doorway.

Therapist: Great, now go over there and be in the mother's space. *(Anna moves over to the place where she has decided the mother's place will be.)*

Anna: Okay, I am the mother now.

Therapist: Mother, how are you?

Mother: I'm good. Yes I'm a good person.

Therapist: I hear that you have a brother-in-law staying with your family at this time.

Mother: Yes, he's such a lovely guy.

Therapist: How does he get on with the kids?

Mother: Oh fine, he's such a lovely guy (*her voice is fading off a little*), such a lovely guy.

Therapist: So everyone's happy when he comes to stay?

Mother: Yes, well um . . . I suppose so. I haven't really thought about that you know. I don't know. I am always so very tired and the kids fight a lot, now that you mention it. They are always whining about one thing or another . . . but I'm sure that it's nothing . . . he's such a lovely guy.

Therapist: Okay now leave the mother space Anna and stand in the middle of the room again. (*Anna gets up from the mother space and walks into the middle of the room, looking thoughtful and shaking her head . . . relieved and confused.*)

Anna: I can't believe it! I was really *her*. That was weird. My head was so cluttered. I could hardly think straight, but I heard what I was saying. She's so stressed, really stressed; like something is seriously wrong but she really can't see it . . .

Therapist: Did you hear what you were saying?

Anna: Yes, he's such a lovely guy.

Therapist: Okay, now go back over to the couch where the child was and be the child again. (*Anna goes over and lies back on the couch and holds the doll. It is only a minute or two before she starts screaming*). Leave me alone! Get me out of here! Make him stop. Make him stop! You stupid fucking bitch make him stop! Get this fucking creep away from me!

Therapist: (*Interrupting abruptly*) Okay, okay . . . leave that place behind and come into this neutral place over here.

Anna: WOW! That was awesome. The feelings are so powerful. She's a killer. That little girl has such strong feelings. She could kill him with her feelings . . . she's so powerful.

Therapist: You are powerful. Let's explore that a little further . . . relax you body and let your mind wander . . . I want you to imagine a large open room, the room where you had an important meeting before you came into this world, before you entered into this life time . . . you may have met with some advisors—or possibly your soul mates, or your angels and your guardians and decided what lessons you would choose for this incarnation. I want you to imagine a room filled with light, white light so brilliant that it soothes your mind . . . Find a large white table and tell me what material the table is made from.

Anna: It's marble, and very cool and smooth to touch.

Therapist: Are there any sounds in the room?

Anna: Yes, I can hear a soothing type of music, not classical but like classical. It's a high frequency soothing sound that I know is music that I have never heard here, but it sounds familiar to me and I feel very comfortable with these sounds near me . . .

Therapist: Is there anyone else in the room?

Anna: Yes, even though it is very bright in here, and there is like a fine mist, I can see a man and he's huge, maybe over six foot tall, like a basketball player only he's a very large American Indian—he has long black hair, some of it is braided in the front and the rest hangs loose down his back. He has a white feather headpiece and other feathers in his hair. I think that he's one of my guides. I can't see his face because he has turned his back on me. I feel he could be friendly if he turned around but he isn't.

Therapist: Ask him to turn around and face you.

Anna: He is very beautiful. He said that I have turned my back on him. He is always with me and he is glad that I am facing him now.

Therapist: Is there anyone else in the room sitting around the table?

Anna: The room sounds and feels alive with lots of people. There's a party atmosphere and all of the people have playing cards in their hands! Instead of hearts, diamonds, spades and clubs, these cards have words to describe experiences on them.

'Hey, you'll love 'poverty,' someone from across the other side of the table yelled, as they threw a card with 'poverty,' written on it, onto the white marble table. It slid across the long table for a couple of feet and then came to a halt. There is silence as the card comes to a stop in the middle of the table. The journey had begun and Anna felt a flutter of excitement and a flush of love run all through her body as the cards began to fly through the air. Anna laughed as she watched the attitude of these people gathered in love for her. She felt loved and appreciated by these people and she felt that she loved them back.

All of these people fully trusted that she could easily handle it all. A female voice shouted playfully.

'Hey, 'physical abuse,' you can do that,'

'That's a good one,' a deep male voice confidently announced.

'Sexual abuse,' that's the most learning. I think let's make it multiple that way you're more likely to really get it!' said a very handsome man on the right side of Anna. He was holding up a clipboard with a list and ticking off each item as it was spoken.

'What about . . . a few car accidents?'

'Hold the phone' . . . a man dressed like a cowboy added excitedly. 'What always spices up the mix is, 'Addiction.' Let's make your parents religious—what's a trip without a whole lot of confusion? And to put icing on that cake—you have to go as a girl this time. It's the only way to travel!'

Therapist: Do you recognise anyone there that has already shown up in your life?

Anna: He's here!
Therapist: Who's there?
Anna: Shane. He just called me 'sweetheart.' He leaned in, gave me a kiss and promised to give me a run for my money . . . what's going on? It's like a play and I chose all the players . . .
Therapist: *How can you trust that you chose this part?*

Aunt

'She's as mad as a cut snake!' Harry said to Anna.
'You're so cruel—she's your sister!'
'She's always been crazy.'
'Really?'
'As long as I can remember.'
'Define crazy!' Anna challenged her father. 'I think that you call a woman crazy when she has a mind of her own. When a woman is doing what she wants to do and not caring what others think—you get nervous—so she has to be crazy.'

'I loved going to the beach house with her for holidays when I was little.'

'The beach house—you mean that shack—she was 'Cracker crazy.' What about that time with the crabs? Your grandfather's house reeked for weeks.'

Anna's Aunty Ella didn't live on a street, she lived on a beach. Not the main beach but further north—you had to drive cross-country in a four-wheel drive to get to it. A few weeks of the school holidays each year at Christmas, Anna stayed with her aunt in a little wood and tin shed on the Queensland coast and roamed wild. Anna remembered one year when she was ten years old she got to stay by herself without her sister or her cousins. She remembered that when she first arrived Ella would make a fuss to make a fire quickly—there was no electricity and she wanted to get it going before it got dark. The house was more like a shack; a tiny dishevelled wooden building with a corrugated iron roof nestled in between a half circle of trees on the edge of the beach. The only dwelling on the whole stretch of sand her family called 'the beach'.

As the sun was going down Aunty Ella grabbed some fishing lines and a towel and started dancing to the portable radio that she had hung around her neck.

'Have you got your dancing feet on beautiful girl?' Ella called out.

'Yeah!' Anna answered not knowing what was happening.

'Come on! We need pipies, bring that bucket with you.' She said pointing at the red bucket on the ground near the water tank as she walked towards the ocean.

'What are pipies?' Anna asked grabbing the bucket and racing after her aunt.

'Pipies, my girl, are little tiny shells that fish love to eat and if we're going to catch fish for our dinner we need them.'

Ella danced all the way down to the water's edge. She pretended to play a piano in front of her syncopating the beat and matching the song. She sang out loud. Anna thought Ella had a beautiful voice and the sounds that she made gave Anna goose bumps.

'When the road gets dark and you can no longer see, just let my love throw a spark and have a little faith in me.' John Hiatt's voice rang out from the radio.

'And when your back's against the wall just turn around and you will see I'll be there, you will see. Have a little faith in me.' Ella sang to Anna smiling and jiving with her joyful comfortable body.

Ella started to do the twist, she moved her hips this way and that and her feet made a hole in the sand that the waves, splashing around her legs, filled in. Ella put her hands into the water and pulled out a handful of pipies that she put into the bucket. Anna watched what Ella did and copied her.

'They're getting away.' Anna squealed laughing at the feeling of the little mussel like shells slipping through her fingers.

'Put your back into it!' Ella said laughing at her niece. 'You have to be quick to grab them or they will burrow deep into the sand to get away from you.' Ella laughed at Anna's efforts.

When they had a few handfuls in the bucket Ella took her off her jeans and shirt and threw them onto her towel. She stood tall in front of Anna in her bikini. She looked fit, strong and happy.

'I'm going for a quick swim and when I get back we'll catch our dinner, OK?'

Ella lifted her feet high and raced across the waves and out into the surf. When the first big wave presented itself blue in front of her, she dived under it with an ease and strength that reminded Anna of a dolphin. She swam out deep into the choppy surf, so far that sometimes Anna could not see her. Eventually Anna spotted her riding a wave with her head and shoulders perched above the white foam, riding it all the way to the shore.

'Let's catch some fish.' Ella said, drying herself off.

No sooner had the pipi shell, hook and line hit the water, Ella was pulling in a fish. It landed on the beach with a loud splat and then it flipped and flopped at Anna's feet for a few seconds before Ella picked it up and put in the bucket.

'Dinner is served!' Ella said cheerfully half an hour later handing Anna a metal plate with steaming fish.

Anna ate the best fish she had ever tasted. Fresh from the sea caught by her favourite aunt. She felt warm and healthy from a good day in the sun and the sea. The flames of the fire danced and crackled as Ella and Anna enjoyed their conversation. The sun had set and the stars were visible and shining overhead. Anna loved the smells, the taste was a delight to her taste buds, her heart felt contented and loved, and sitting around that fireplace she felt home.

Anna fell to sleep in her hammock listening to the waves smash onto the shore. Each morning Anna would jump up and throw some pinecones on the fireplace. It was not long before the embers jumped to life and crackled into flames. Anna knew how to make her own breakfast. She got a piece of white bread and pierced it in the middle with the big black metal fork and held it close to the flames to brown.

Wild brumby horses grazed on the grass outside the back door of their little shack. They were so tame that Anna could pat them and plait seashells into their manes, and feed them carrots, bread and sugar cubes. Sometimes they followed her down to the water's edge to watch her swim. In the mornings, before Ella woke up, Anna walked on the beach exploring. She found starfish, seashells and gnarly driftwood walking sticks that doubled as a sword or a magic wand.

One day huge clumps of salty seaweed littered the waterline, next day the seaweed had disappeared completely and in its place blue bottles scattered across the sand like puffed up balloons. Each day a different coastline presented itself and Anna roamed alone, immersed and fascinated. On windy days Anna would roll a towel around her leg making a sausage circle and then place the circle on top of her head. The towel encircled her body like her own private change room. She would make an opening for her face and the rest of her towel would fall down her back so that she looked like an Arab sheik, or the queen of her desert with sand in her hair, in her clothes and in between her teeth.

'We have to go to Shelly beach and get shells for my aunts.' Ella said making a coffee for her and sitting in front of the fire.

'I love that beach.'

'Are you going to help me find shells today?'

'Yes, I bet you that I'll find the most.'

'We want cowries Anna.'

Anna loved all shells, the cluster winks, abalones, coral shells and even the creepers. She liked cowries too but she found them hard to find.

'The aunties want cowries! It's like money to them because they make things out of them and sell to the tourists.'

'How do you find so many cowries?' Anna said looking at the basket full on the bench.

'Cowrie shells are smooth and shiny—I like the big ones so I look for that dark brown speckled colour on the top.' Ella said holding the shell out to show Anna.

'That's what I have been looking for but I still can't find them.' Anna said disappointed.

Ella picked up another cowry shell, 'they are white on the bottom and egg-shaped. See the flat under surface which shows a long, narrow, slit-like opening which is toothed at the edges, like its going to eat you?' Ella joked pushing the shell towards Anna's face.

'No get it away from me!' Shrieked Anna—'they do look like teeth!'

'They are beautiful, not scary. Look, its like a smiley face!' Ella said, holding the shell up into the light. 'All cowries have that porcelain-like shine.'

'Why do you only want those ones?'

'Cowries have been used for centuries as a currency in Africa, India and China. Huge amounts of cowries were introduced into Africa by western nations during the slave trade. Starting over three thousand years ago, cowry shells, or copies of the shells, have been used as a means of exchange. The aboriginal people used cowry shells in sacred ceremonies as a symbol of womanhood, fertility, birth and wealth and your great aunts make pretty stuff with them.'

'Okay I'll look harder.'

'Maybe look for the white side of the shell—it really does look like a smiley face.' Ella said holding the shells with the smile facing towards Anna.

The next day the waves receded quickly and Ella pulled Anna around the rocks into the cove that was Shelley beach. Anna had thongs on and her feet slipped and slid with the shifting surface of shells beneath her feet. Anna fell to her knees and started digging with her hands. No matter how deep she went there were shells. Shells so deep that she couldn't find an end to them.

She watched her aunt picking out shells and placing them in a canvas bag over her shoulder. Anna looked down at the ground and there right in front of her was a big white smiley face—the biggest cowry she had ever seen.

'I found one!'

'Excellent girl!' Ella shouted over the sound of the waves. 'Keep looking.'

Smiley faces kept appearing for over an hour and each one Anna picked up brought a bigger smile to her face. The tide was rising quickly. Anna could feel the water rising around her knees now and feel the pull of the water out to sea.

'We have to go now' Ella said lugging her bag.

When they got back to the shack Ella wanted to load the car with the shells and get organised to stay a few days at her parent's house.

'Go play for a bit and I will call you when I'm ready to go.' Ella instructed.

Anna went walking with the red bucket down to the water. She caught three large crabs with the bucket and dragged it along the sand to show Ella.

When they arrived at the main house Anna asked her aunt to help her lift the bucket down onto the ground, she wanted to show her grandfather. Ella lifted it down for her before walking inside.

'Don't you let them out of that bucket.'

'No I won't.'

Anna put her hand into the water and tried to pick a crab up from behind like she had seen Ella do. She lifted one of the crabs out of the bucket and then it snapped its claw at her, nipping her fingers. She dropped it on the grass outside the house and it quickly disappeared under the house, scampering sideways. Anna chased after it diving onto the grass out in front of her but it had gone.

'What's up?' Ella said on her way out to the car.

'Nothing.' Anna said feeling a little bit guilty.

'Don't you let those crabs loose now will you?'

'No.' Anna called out to her aunt as Ella walked back into the house with her arms full of pillows and sleeping bags.

Anna went to the car to get her backpack out. As she pulled it down from the seat her backpack swung down and knocked the bucket over and the remaining two crabs scampered over the grass and under the house. When Ella came outside to see what Anna was doing she looked at her in horror when she saw Anna lying on her belly looking under the house.

'Where are the crabs?'

'They ran under there.'

'Oh no! You are going to be so popular. Have you ever smelt a dead crab?'

'Are they going to die?' Anna asked, getting upset now.

'Well they're not going to come when you call them and I'm not climbing under there.'

'We're leaving first thing in the morning!'

'Why?'

'Because those crabs will stink to high heaven and you won't be very popular.'

'Really?'

'Yes and they will never forget that we came to visit!'

'That beach shack was the best childhood memories I ever had.'

'That beach shack needed bulldozing.' Harry said with a smirk across his face.

'I love her and I think that she's awesome!'

'You would—you're a lot like her.'

'And anyway the crabs were my fault—she just never told on me.'

'I rest my case.'

'Whenever I think of her I feel happy. I think that she was such a free spirit!'

Dance

Anna was running late for her dance class. She grabbed an apple from the fruit bowl on the kitchen bench and took a bite. She threw her bag over her shoulder and pulled the front door of her house closed behind her. When she looked up she noticed her car in the driveway was wide open. All four doors of her car were open wide. The glove box was open and the papers were strewn all over the front seat.

'Oh no!' Anna said out loud to herself as she pulled herself into the driver's seat—the centre section of the back seat had been pulled forward and some of the contents from the boot were pulled into the car.

She sat for a moment stunned; she nearly jumped out of the car to call the police. But, instead, took a deep breath, and considered that now she was even later for her class. She opened the ashtray and was surprised to see a twenty-dollar note was still there from the night before.

'What exactly is missing?' she asked out loud to herself as she put her seat belt on. 'Maybe nothing's missing.'

It was beginning to rain as she put the key in the ignition and started the car. She thought about who might have broken into her car. Anna drove to her class a little numb. When she arrived the others had already begun dancing. She acknowledged her dance teacher, Meesha, with a nod and took a long sip from her water bottle. Anna pulled off her running shoes and walked barefoot into the centre of the dance floor. Six other dancers were scattered on the floor stretching and moving about to the rhythms of the music.

Anna smiled at Meesha as she started to dance and join in with the class . . .

'Welcome Anna!' Meesha said in her friendly way. 'I was just telling everyone how Gabrielle Roth designed the power wave dance and its five rhythms to allow the motion of the body to heal you, inspire and change you . . . and we will now begin today to dance the five rhythms.

'Let's dance the first rhythm, staccato,' Meesha shouted loudly over the music to the whole studio. 'Staccato is fiery and percussive, it's angles and action like karate kicks and chops, cutting through, slicing the air about you—Staccato!'

Anna watched Meesha jump around the room like a karate master, kicking sharply with her legs and feet and chopping with her arms.

'Dance . . . move your bodies everyone, the whole point is embodiment! We're all on a trip . . . we're stuck in a mind trip . . . disconnected from our centre. Disconnected from our ancestors, disconnected from our genius . . . our movement holds us. Our movement rocks us and shapes us as human beings . . . as human beings our natural nature is motion, it's spontaneous and it's original. We have lost that and we have to retrieve our souls . . . dance will bring you back to your centre.'

'Good, that's it . . . you've got it!' Meesha spoke clearly to the whole group to be heard over the music. 'Let's move on to Flowing.'

Anna loved this class, and wondered where her energy was coming from. The more she danced, the more energy she seemed to have.

Meesha was dancing around the room as she spoke to the class. She was animated and alive. 'Flowing . . . it's grounding you . . . the movements are receptive and circular . . . it's feminine movement,' Meesha spoke in a softer voice and moved with fluid lines as she spoke.

Anna danced in the flowing rhythm and into her mind came the thoughts of her car as she moved her body . . . she was thinking in her head and it occurred to her that she had not told anyone of her dramatic story—her car had been broken into and she might have been robbed.

The music changed to an Aboriginal soundtrack. The didgeridoo vibrations flowed through Anna's body and she closed her eyes and went with the flow. Her body felt loose and easy as sweat trickled down her chest between her breasts. She lowered her body into a semi squat, grounding herself more, stomping her feet—in a similar way to the aboriginal dancers she had seen so many times. The click of the rhythm sticks, the sound of didgeridoo and her feet stomping onto the floor in a tribal beat lifted her body into a trance deeper and deeper into her centre. In her mind's eye, like a movie, she saw three aboriginal children.

She saw them sitting in her car—sorting through her stuff—a girl with long brown hair and beautiful brown friendly eyes and two young boys—one smaller and one taller than the girl . . .

'Wow! They are so little!' Anna thought to herself. Suddenly she was not afraid anymore. She didn't need to be, she felt compassion and she could see that these kids were probably looking for money—they just didn't think to look in her ashtray.

'Chaos is a deep letting go!' Meesha instructed, from the front of the room, changing the music again. 'Chaos is the energy of the child . . . in the moment.'

Anna felt liberated, as she moved in the chaos rhythm—wild, and uninhibited, dancing out the stiffness in her muscles, dancing away the fears in her mind, dancing away the sadness in her heart, dancing up a new childlike joy in her body that was delicious and fun.

'Excellent, now let's go back to Staccato. It's percussive and fiery . . . it's a more masculine movement . . . the gateway to trance . . .'

Anna liked the Staccato rhythm the best. She was sure that she must have been a man, even a Samurai in a past life. She could jump high and feel the surging freedom in her bones.

'Lyrical is focusing on the linear . . . it's connected to spirit— whatever that is for you!' Meesha's voice softened, as did her body.

Anna found this one the hardest. She thought it was girly and her body seemed to tense up a little whenever she attempted this Lyrical movement.

'Dance is being who you are in the moment . . . nobody else can dance your dance. *Where in your body, does trust live?*' Meesha instructed the dancers as she sorted through the large CD collection near her stereo at the front of the room.

'Now stop. You can stay standing or lay down on the floor . . . stillness is the return to emptiness . . . let each of the rhythms invoke your spirit.' Meesha talked quite softly now, as she lowered herself to the floor.

Anna had danced her body into a state of deep peaceful calm and as she lowered her own body to the floor, she had to ask herself the question—did the dramatic story create itself or did she create it . . . could she trust the stories that she was telling herself . . . or was something else occurring?

Grandmother

The grand clock stood like a sentinel in Mara's dining room. Growing up, Anna loved the constant, reliable, ticking of her grandmother's clock. It sounded on the hour; 'ding, dong,' winding, winding and then a soothing, 'tick-tock, tick-tock.' The rich, dark polished wood of the clock matched dining table and chairs. It was furniture made to last.

Anna liked its round friendly face and she would make up games and funny dance movements to join in with the ding-dong on the hour ding-dong. Winding, winding, winding. The tick, tock and the sounds of the clock were regular and constant and Anna liked that.

'What are you doing?' asked Mara, obviously irritated.
'Nothing.'
'Don't touch that!'
'I didn't.'
'I can see your finger prints all over it!'
'I didn't.'
'Don't touch anything!'
'I wouldn't touch it!'
'Be quiet, look there—you've left your finger prints all over that.'
'No I didn't.'
'You're enough to send anyone crazy!'

'I wish you were dead, you big fat old lady,' Anna thought to herself as she gave her grandmother an evil stare. 'I wish you were dead. I wish you were dead. I wish you were dead. Die! Die, I wish you would go away from me forever.'

Anna called her 'Granny,' but contrary to what that word evokes—a frail, lovely, little old lady—her grandmother was GRANNY, a big round force of a woman. Mara was so fat that her bottom filled the lounge chair—whenever she stood up—the chair would have to slowly drop off her backside. She was so fat—that the skin on the back of her arms rolled over the arms of the chair, as she sat there knitting.

'Pat, pat, pat.'

'What are you doing?'

'I'm patting all of the fat wobbly skin on the back of your arms!'

'Why on earth are you doing that?'

'It wobbles!'

'Get out from behind there or I'll belt you.'

'Pat, pat, pat, pat.' was the sound Anna was making on her grandmother's arm.

'What are you doing?'

'I'm patting the skin under your arm, its fat and wobbly,' Anna said, as a matter of fact.

'Why?'

'It feels good.'

'Stop it.'

'I'm not hurting anything,' Anna argued.

'Stop it now.'

'I don't want to—I'm not leaving any finger prints.'

'You'll be hurting in a minute—you are so infuriating!' yelled Mara, as she turned to take a swipe at Anna, interrupting her knitting, but Anna knew to stay out of reach.

Mara loved knitting, moss and cable stitch: every day, and every night, the needles clicked together, as she continued to knit at a rapid rate. Uncles, aunts, sisters, brothers and cousins all had jumpers, courtesy of Mara.

Besides knitting, Mara had mastered cooking. She made lamingtons, fairy cakes, trifle, jelly and custard. Another of her specialties was Christmas pudding with sixpences that stuck on the roof of your mouth. She made old-fashioned dumplings and roast chicken, which were always served with big brown bottles of beer.

Anna remembered . . . her grandmother's long hair—it fell down past her bottom. She plaited it tightly and wrapped around her head in coils. Tess, her sister, was allowed to brush her hair at night, but Anna wasn't. Tess was allowed to sleep in her grandmother's bed but Anna never was. She remembered drunken laughter and shouting, the narrow dimly lit stairway, and up the stairs on the second floor was the darkness. Anna was afraid of the dark, she was afraid of the rattling louvered windows and the cold whistling wind.

Anna lived in between her grandparents. Her grandfather, Ronald lived at the top of the street and her grandmother Mara, lived at the bottom. Sometimes they shared breakfast but the reconciliation rarely lasted until morning tea. Pots would fly as Mara expressed her frustration. Ronald would snatch Anna up into his arms and dash out the front door, away to his house.

Mara's front fence was a row of steel spears—held together in the middle by a steel railing. The fence looked strong and secure and safe, as if it could keep the bad out. Anna remembered getting her head stuck in that fence. A big friendly fireman with a husky voice came to rescue her. He rubbed butter all around her ears and head to get it slippery and then held her shoulders softly and pulled her head out . . . Anna got her head stuck in that fence . . .

'Not you again!' the fireman laughed as he arrived at the house to free Anna again . . . he rubbed butter all around her head and ears to get it slippery and then held her shoulders and pulled her head out . . . Anna got her head stuck in between those fence posts again and again.

'You are a stupid little girl . . . such a stupid little girl. Maybe we should just leave you there this time.'

Mara would sometimes come to stay at Anna's house and Anna didn't like that one bit. Once when Anna was seven years old, she went on a sleepover at her friend Katie's house. Katie was Italian with a very large family, only she didn't have a mother—her mother had died when Katie was a baby—Anna was relieved to get away from her Granny.

The two girls had a fun day playing outside and then Katie's father called them in for dinner. The family made a great fuss of Anna as their guest. They made her sit at the end of the table. There were a few aunts but mostly uncles and grandparents, lots of little kids, and Anna and Katie. When everyone was seated at the table, they brought out the dinner and placed a big plate in front of Anna. For a seven-year old girl, the plate was huge. A steaming bed of rice topped with chicken—the bottom part of the chicken—not his legs—the parson's nose. The chicken was sitting on her plate, cooked to a golden brown. Anna looked up from the plate and all of her guests were looking at her wide-eyed and happy. Anna looked back to her plate and then at her friend.

Italian language flowed over her as they had a conversation
'Do you like chicken?' Katie asked.
'Usually I do,' answered Anna.

They held out their hands and clasped Anna's, making a circle around the table. Grace was said in Italian, thanking God for the gifts before them.

Anna was relieved by the diversion and yet transfixed by the meal in front of her—speechless. All eyes were again on her, as the family waited for their guest to begin eating.

'Is there something wrong?' asked Katie, when Anna looked at her even more uncomfortable than before. She looked at her uncle and shrugged her shoulders.

The tension in the room was growing. This seven-year old visitor was responsible for everyone's dinner getting progressively colder. Anna couldn't bring herself to take a bite of this meal. She couldn't jump up and run away because it was night-time and too far from her own house. Feeling trapped, she let out a nervous giggle. And then she laughed a little more and looked around the room helplessly, and then they all started laughing, the uncles, aunties, cousins and grandparents, were all laughing now. Anna had tears running down her cheeks because she was laughing so much, holding her cramping stomach. A wave of energy washed around the table connecting them in laughter. When the wave subsided, the uncle shaking his head and laughing still, removed Anna's dinner and went to the kitchen, and returned with a fresh green salad.

ೲೲೲೲ

When Anna returned home from the sleepover she found out Mara was ill. Harry called an ambulance and they took her to the hospital. She remembers the smell of her grandmother and the smell of the hospital. Sitting on a bench in the hospital room, Anna watched while her father fussed about Mara, puffing her pillow and pouring her a drink of lemonade.

'Where is your suit?' Mara asked Harry.

'It's forty in the shade, Mum, I'm not wearing a suit when it's forty in the shade!'

'You should have worn your suit to take me to the hospital. What will people think?'

Her father wore checked shorts, a white polo shirt and 'Old Spice' aftershave. Anna thought he had really curly hair on his legs and his shorts looked funny. She sat on the floor next to his legs and pulled the hairs to see how long they were when she stretched them out.

'Stop that!' Harry said, pushing her away with his leg.

Mara looked at her in irritation. Anna looked into her grandmother's face. She knew that her Granny was scared and she wished that her Granny were dead.

Coaching

'Look at the board now.' Nadia directed the audience as she wrote, 'Are you 'at cause' in your life or 'at the effect' of it?' in blue chalk on the blackboard. Her smooth Russian accent rolled off her tongue. 'Which question best describes how you live your life?' she asked. She waited a few minutes for her audience to ponder her question before she continued.

'By being 'at the effect' a person experiences emotional problems happening *to* them, rather than being something that happens by them. A person 'at the effect,' will seek treatment rather than seek change. Questions such as, 'Will this work for me?' or statements such as, 'It didn't work for me.' Or, 'it worked for a day and then the problem came back.' Presuppose that the problem and the NLP process are one hundred percent responsible and that the person is themselves, zero percent responsible for their own results.

The positive intention of 'at the effect,' responses is to explain what is happening without being at fault, but by allowing for the possibility of their responses affecting their internal experience. The person makes it impossible to change their experience.

Neurolinguistic Programming is the study of happy successful people by Richard Bandler and John Grinder. What they found is that happy successful people know how to use their mind, body and environment to get the results that they want. The mind and life is a system. When we set goals, we change the mind and physiology towards achieving that outcome and in this way they are 'at cause,' and life happens the way they choose it to happen.'

'Well obviously I'm, 'at the effect,' said the frail man seated next to Anna.

'If you are not fully 'at cause,' you are 'at the effect,' of your emotions or your environment and allowing life to happen to you,' Nadia continued.

'Oh!' he said, surprised. Anna smiled at him warmly.

'The unconscious mind or the soul has access to all of the lived experience of the individual, with all of the sensory information attached. We now know, and science confirms this, that the foundations for mental health, creativity and the capacity to love begin before birth. From the moment of conception, the unborn baby experiences the thoughts and emotions of the mother, as well as its own and these, then impact the baby's development. Every judgment becomes like an already, always listening—a preoccupation with past thoughts that defines how that child sees and experiences the world that they live in.' Nadia stopped momentarily, brushed her blond, wavy hair off her face, and allowed her audience time to absorb what she was saying.

'I know that this is right, I've actually remembered stuff from my womb experience,' Anna whispered to her friend sitting in the row in front of her.

'As adults, consciously we may envision happiness, wealth and love for ourselves while we focus our consciousness on happy thoughts, but the unconscious mind has been recording each and every judgment, from the very beginning. How is the unconscious going to move us forward and manage our affairs? Precisely however it was programmed in the womb and in early childhood. Eighty-five percent of the neural pathways in the brain are formed by the time a child is seven years old. Most people are not even aware that these thoughts and feelings are acting for them automatically,' Nadia continued.

'Oh my God, my family was really screwed up back then. Come to think of it my family is still screwed up!' Anna joked out loud to the woman sitting next to her.

'The good news is that when you break all matter down . . . you get light energy. Everything that exists is light . . . everything that you can sense or feel are patterns of light. When you identify the problem state, and give it a mark of intensity out of ten—zero is no intensity, ten is full intensity—then you have quantified the pattern. Everything you can feel, see or sense with any of the senses is a sensation in the body, coupled with a thought form. It's a pattern of energy. Once you bring awareness to the situation, it can change. You are light, and light can be manipulated.' Nadia said, looking at the front row of students.

'A person could have millions of negative thoughts!' Anna spoke directly to Nadia.

'Yes, you're right, a person could have lots and lots and this is how they can change them easily. It's like this,' Nadia moved closer to Anna and spoke directly to the front row of the audience. 'The very first time a person experienced an emotional hurt, it sets up a way of perceiving and experiencing the world that is not absolutely true. From that time onwards, they would refer to that experience, unconsciously of course, and see only experiences that match the past. In a similar way a pebble thrown into a pond, causes waves that ripple and flow out, beyond the pebble. That thought about the hurt, sets the world of that person on a course of travel,' Nadia stopped talking for a moment and looked around the room for a response.

'But that could take a lifetime to change all of those thoughts back to positive!' Anna said exasperated.

'Or not! Big changes can occur with just a little focus and attention,' Nadia said, smiling a beautiful smile. 'So in order to find the original experience we need to breathe and relax and think of a limiting situation. Ask the unconscious mind to float back over your life experience to the time when the cycle began, to the thought that was 'the pebble,' that stopped your flow in this area, or made you separate, in this particular way.' Nadia spoke with such authority that every one in the room was totally fascinated by her.

'What we are going to be doing in a moment, is to get into pairs. One person becomes aware of a specific problem, and the other person leads them through this process. Okay!'

'How can we do this?' A tall man in the front row asked.

'I'm going to show you. Listen and be aware of a negative pattern in your life now. If I could feel this problem somewhere in my body, where would it be? Breathe and be still! Pay attention to where your attention moves in your body. Wherever your attention shows up in your body is the right place. If it had a shape, what shape would it be? If it had a colour, what colour would it be? If it had a texture, what texture would it be? Become aware of that energy as the pattern in your body . . . now move your attention to the edges of that pattern . . . outside of that area, where the pattern does not exist. Move your attention outside of where you feel or sense that pattern in your body.' Nadia's voice was soft and comforting, lulling the audience into a state of calm.

'Notice how outside differs from inside. Take your attention outside of your body. Know that light energy is the same outside as it is inside. Light energy is all around us and also inside us. Consider that there is no separation. You are light.' Nadia said in a soothing voice. 'Finally breathe into your body as a whole, on your inhale, filling your body completely, and breathe out emptying your body on your exhale, and this time breathe in and smile from you heart,

Reclaiming Trust

filling your body with a smile of love, appreciation and trust. As you exhale send that loving smile out to every cell of your body.' Nadia finished speaking and picked up a pile of papers from the desk at the side of the room.

'That sounds good to me.' said a woman in the front row. Nadia looked around the room.

'Are there any questions?' Nadia asked pulling up a chair and facing the audience.

'What if nothing comes to mind?' A redheaded woman in the back called out.

'Your unconscious mind is your genius. It has been with you from your beginning. How can it not know?' Nadia replied sounding like a sage.

'I don't believe that I can do that,' another man on the aisle seat said.

'In a moment you can have a go and see for yourself, just let me finish showing your how to do it.' Nadia requested pleasantly, patting him on the shoulder.

'We all store time in different ways . . . and your unconscious mind stored the event in the time it occurred, with the resources that you had at that time. Attention to the cycle of thoughts to release negative emotions from the past does not mean that you will never feel that emotion again. It means that the negative judgment that caused separation is no longer there. Is that something that would be of interest to you?' Nadia said, walking up the aisle towards the back of the room.

'It sounds a bit too simple.'

'It is not simple, it is like a circle, a negative thought or judgment about the world will keep returning from experience to the original thought, creating itself again and again in order to heal or resolve itself.' Nadia finished speaking and handed instructions out to the front row. The room was a buzz of chatter with all of the students talking to each other, excited about the learning that this technique would bring.

'Find a partner and let's begin this learning.'

Anna and a tall redheaded woman moved towards each other.

'My name is Tracy,' she said, shaking Anna's hand to introduce herself.

'Hi.' Anna responded warmly, pulling her seat towards Tracy and sitting down.

'Have you done this before?' Tracy asked tentatively moving over a little before sitting down.

'You want to go first, Anna?' Tracy asked.

'Okay.'

'Let's establish which pattern you want to change and then we will begin.'

Anna thought about what pattern or limiting thought she wanted to change.

'What is the pattern or limiting thought that you want to change?' Tracy asked, reading directly from the page in the instruction manual.

'A lot of times I feel stupid and I don't know where that comes from.' Anna said, feeling stupid and smiling to herself.

'Okay, so now would it be alright with your unconscious mind for you to release the beginning of that cycle of limitation and for you to be aware of it?'

'Yes that would be okay, I suppose.'

'Great, let's do that then. Close your eyes and take a big breath in, and as you exhale think of the circle of thoughts that 'I'm stupid is attached to,' Tracy said, following the process as best she could.

Anna had a number of memories come to mind around the thought, 'I'm stupid.'

'Okay, if that thought of 'feeling stupid' had a shape, what shape would it be? Tracy asked

'A circle.'

'If it had a colour . . . what colour would it be?'

'Red.'

'Now that you are aware of that old thought pattern—move your awareness outside to the edge of that pattern.'

'Okay,' said Anna.

'Now move your awareness outside of your body and notice where the pattern is not. Look back at the pattern and notice it changing as your awareness grows. Allow that 'I'm stupid,' pattern to change completely.' Tracy said.

She was sitting on a chair, at a forty-five degree angle to Tracy. Anna's eyes were closed and in her imagination she floated outside the pattern. Suddenly she began to think of her grandfather and a time when she was very young. In her mind she saw her grandfather holding her and walking down the road towards her grandmother's house. Anna had a feeling of great love for her grandfather, so intense that she lost any sense of herself. She merged into her grandfather and became part of him. Then in her mind, she saw her grandmother standing in front of both of them and looking at her in a way that confused her at first.

'Oh my God!'

'What's happening?' Tracy asked quickly.

'She's looking at me in a strange way, a very strange way, at first I didn't understand it because I was so little and I just realised she's not trusting me.'

'What do you mean?'

'She doesn't trust me with my grandfather.' Anna said and realised, at that moment, that when she was so little her grandmother looked at her like she was the other woman. Her grandmother was jealous of her. That was when Anna had decided about herself that she must not be trustworthy.

'Oh my God, I can't be trusted!' Anna said out loud.

'Why can't you be trusted?'

'My grandmother sees me as the other woman. Oh my God! She *knew* that he was abusing me and she blamed me instead of helping me. My grandmother was jealous of me, like I got in between her and him, like I took him from her.'

'How old are you?' Tracy said.

'I'm little, so very little, that's its so ridiculous, it's funny. But it makes so much sense to me.'

'What do you need to learn from outside of this pattern—the learning of which will allow you to let go of the belief—'I'm stupid,' effortlessly?'

'I was trying so hard to get myself help. It felt so wrong! They were not responding properly. I had all of these memories in my head that never made sense to me—weird memories like, sticking my head in the fence and getting it stuck over and over again. I remembered her burning my hand on the stove, because she didn't want me to tell anyone. Somehow, because I couldn't understand what was going on—I decided that I must be stupid.' Anna slumped back in her seat. Her mind was reeling with pain and relief at the same time. 'I need to learn that I am smart now, and that I was way smart then. I am trustworthy. I can be trusted. It was my grandparents that were not worthy of my trust. Instead of helping me, my grandmother blamed me. God! She was the adult—I am innocent and she needed to help me and keep me safe. My grandfather needed to guard my innocence, not take it away from me.'

'That is a great learning Anna,' Tracy said, with warmth and compassion in her voice.

'Is there anything else that you understand now that you are outside of that pattern looking back on it?'

'Yes! Sexual abuse is not acceptable! It's not going to go away while everyone is ignoring it. It is not an individual problem, or a separate family problem, or even a single race problem: it's a humankind problem. We need to treat our children and their childhood as precious, and absolutely *SACRED!*'

'Wow that's intense incredible learning,' Tracy said with tears rolling down her face.

'Lets take a big breathe before we continue.'

'This is awesome, lets keep going!' Anna said sitting on the edge of her seat.

'Okay, have you got another limiting thought pattern that you want to change?' Tracy asked.

'Life is dangerous!'

'Okay, if that thought, 'life is dangerous,' had a shape, what shape would it be?

'A triangle,'

'If it had a colour . . . what colour would it be?'

'Black,'

'Now that you are aware of that old thought pattern—move your awareness outside to the edge of that pattern.'

'Okay,' said Anna.

'Now move your awareness outside of your body and notice where the pattern is not. Look back at the pattern and notice it changing as your awareness grows. Allow that, 'life is dangerous,' pattern to change completely.' Tracy said.

'I'm feeling sick.'

'You are doing great, notice what else is happening.'

'It was before my birth.'

'Was it in the womb or a past life?' Tracy asked, intrigued with the information that was coming from Anna.

'It was in the womb.'

'How many months in the womb?'

'Four months.'

'Okay,' Tracy prompted. 'What else?'

'I want to die. I'm too afraid to be born and I want to die!'

'Okay, Ask your unconscious mind what it needs to understand and learn from outside of that pattern, and your unconscious mind can preserve the learning so that if you need it in the future it will be there,' Tracy said.

'People are trying to kill me and stopping me from doing what I want.'

'Who's trying to kill you?' Tracy asked.

'The doctors during my mother's pregnancy, they stitched me in and I couldn't do what I wanted to do.'

'Doctors like to save people—do they not? Were they really trying to kill you?

'They were stitching me in—they were trying it out as an experiment.'

'So you are saying that a team of doctors, a team of specialist doctors, were trying a new and innovative procedure to keep you alive.'

'Yes but it felt like they were trying to kill me.'

'They were working to save you—like you were such a precious soul that they went to great lengths to help you stay alive.'

'Oh! That's a new perspective. I've always felt that I had to brace myself against the evil people trying to stop me from doing what I wanted. It was like my infant brain put the feelings of helplessness together with the hurt and just felt like a victim. When you put it that way it makes sense in such a wonderful way. It feels so good just to think about it that way—I have goose bumps,' said Anna.

'Yes and if you were meant to die, you would have died, I think. You were meant to live,' Tracy said.

'I have never thought of it in that way before but it is very true that they saved my life.'

'It sounds like they pulled all of their resources and new cutting edge technology together to keep you alive and bring you into this world safely and with great care. That is a wonderful learning. Breathe in that new perspective and feel the grace in that learning— You are smiling—that is good . . . allow that smile to flow into every cell of your awareness now. *I wonder what you have to fix or change now to trust yourself fully?*'

Fairytale

So as the story went, Anna realised that she was so much more than her mind. She had minded her mind and along the way she had told herself many stories; happy stories, sad stories, frightening stories, and each story had left its mark on her mind. The stories she told herself left her with misconceptions about herself, misconceptions about the world that she was living in and how her life occurred to her. She realised that the world that she was living in had become, what she thought it was, before she was ever aware that she was taking any notice.

One night before she went to sleep she opened the hatch when no one was watching; she climbed down into the tunnel that was there in her imagination, going into the opening in the earth, deeper and deeper into the centre.

The earth felt like a mother to her, inviting her deeper inside, deeper beneath the surface. The tunnel was lined with thick gnarly vines. She supported her own weight and climbed down the steep hollow by hanging onto the vines and lowering herself, swinging like a monkey from one vine to the next. The deeper she climbed, the safer she felt. The deeper she climbed into the earth, the more relaxed she became. Eventually, she heard the sound of silence and intuitively she knew that she had arrived. Anna let go and gravity held her like love; it held her like a trusted friend and she landed on her feet.

Anna landed in the snow, knee deep. As far as she could see for miles around, soft, white encircled her in all directions. Her hooded jacket, leggings, boots and mittens were made from caribou. The inner layer of fur touched her skin, and the outer layer of fur captured the heat of her body keeping her warm. Anna felt nurtured and nourished. Pure, white snow shimmered quietly, in the sunlight. Suddenly, a sound startled Anna and she quickly turned to find a magnificent, white polar bear standing behind her. The bear was huge. He stood on all four of his thick legs and he towered over Anna.

'Climb on,' he said in a soft soothing voice.

Anna awkwardly climbed up onto the bear's back; she sat astride his shoulders like she might ride a horse.

'I want to tell you something,' the polar bear said.

Anna was so excited: she was climbing up onto the back of a big white bear.

'Hold on a minute,' she said shifting her weight. She moved around to get comfortable until eventually she lay on her stomach. Her arms dropped down around his neck and she hugged the bear from there.

'Listen very carefully,' he said in a soft tone.

'What is it?' Anna questioned.

'Allow.'

'Allow what?'

'Allow your higher self.' The polar bear repeated, ceremoniously standing still for a moment.

'Okay,' she heard herself say out loud—more like a question than anything else. The bear walked on through the snow, rocking Anna as he went. Soon she drifted off to sleep.

Anna didn't know how long she slept or where the bear was going, but when she woke up and she sat up straight and looked around. All she could see, in every direction, was the purest white. For for the longest time, Anna sat silently, and the bear walked along. Anna pondered the bear's words, 'Allow your higher self.' Sitting elevated on the bear's back she realized, that she had always looked outside of herself to feel better about herself. Sitting high on the bear's back feeling comfortable and warm, she felt grace now—she had minded her mind yesterday and today—she knew how important it was to mind her mind for tomorrow and she felt grace in her heart. She felt goodness inside her body—and the same grace and goodness outside of her body, and she named that feeling trust.

Anna felt very comfortable being so close to him that she could feel his heart beat. The bear walked majestically through the snow, his paws softly sinking into the snow, rocking her ever so gently. Anna felt safe and innocent. She snuggled into the warm soft fur of her polar bear and once again, she drifted off to sleep.

ANNA

At lunchtime the Neurolinguistic Programming and Hypnosis training group went outside to get lunch at the various cafes in town. It was a beautiful summer's day and Anna enjoyed walking through the shopping mall with her new friends. She felt better in herself, somehow she felt different; more present in the way she connected and communicated with people.

For the last few minutes of lunch she sat in the park outside the hotel and soaked up the sunshine. Everyone gathered in the foyer area. Some people were seated at the table, others stood up and the conversation was enthusiastic and friendly. The group slowly filtered back into the seminar room and Anna moved to join them.

Troy came back from lunch with his wife Danielle, pushing their one-year old daughter, Charlie in her stroller. He wheeled the stroller to a stop, next to Anna, who was bobbed down, adjusting her right shoe. Anna looked up to see Charlie peering at her with a big smile and a curious glance. The little girl tilted her head to the left and smiled. Anna mirrored Charlie's physical action and tilted her head. Charlie smiled again, and moved her head to the other side maintaining eye contact with Anna all the while. When Anna mirrored Charlie's second movement, Charlie held her hand up and pointed her finger towards Anna, just like in the movie 'E.T,' the Extraterrestrial pointed at Elliot before he boarded the spaceship to go home. Anna held her finger out in an identical way and the moment the tips of their fingers met, Charlie laughed with delight.

Troy noticed their interaction and he smiled down at Charlie with love and amusement. The conversations in the room got louder for a moment and Anna's attention was drawn back to the group. But when she looked back to Charlie a few minutes later, Charlie moved her head in the same way again and Anna mirrored her. She matched her again by holding her pointing finger out and touching Charlie's finger tip to tip as if the process needed repeating. Anna laughed out loud with Charlie this time and considered how enlightened this little being was—so innocent and full of trust. Anna felt herself fill with love and light and acknowledgement that she was once like this beautiful little girl in front of her—innocent, lovable and completely intelligent.

Troy walked back into the seminar room and stood on the stage up the front while everyone came back to their seats. He looked refreshed and full of energy. Anna waived goodbye to Charlie and her mother as they left.

'Okay people back to work.'

Each time Anna returned to the chair she seemed to allow herself to go deeper . . . to notice what a pleasure it is to do nothing here . . .

'It really doesn't matter . . .' Troy began speaking in his most soothing hypnotic voice. 'That today is a new day, a day you've never experienced before, because today you can rediscover whichever of your previous powers or abilities you would like in order to relax completely . . . in this place, here . . . and there . . . where you have been relaxed before now . . . drifting and listening and hearing, about how comfortable you can be . . . ' Troy stopped talking for a moment to allow quiet in the room.

'Let the unconscious mind give to the conscious mind whatever it needs to know, let the unconscious mind give to the conscious mind whatever it needs to change, let the unconscious mind give to the conscious mind whatever it needs to do to fix whatever it needs to fix . . .' he said.

Anna was still sitting in the second row feeling deeply relaxed and not at all bothered or even aware of how long she had been sitting in the chair.

'In a moment you will come back into the room feeling refreshed, as if you've had a full night's sleep—I am going to count from one to five and with each ascending number you will feel good about yourself and the changes that you have made now. With each breath you take, and in the spaces in between each ascending number, you will begin to feel the circulation and the energy increasing in your body, bringing feelings of health and joyfulness. Five . . . feeling confident in the changes that you have made for yourself with the help of hypnosis . . . four . . . allowing these profound healing changes to somehow go deep into your healing mind where they will work automatically whenever you need them to . . . over the days and weeks and months ahead . . . three . . . noticing the quality of relaxation in your body now and knowing that you can create that for yourself any time you wish . . . two . . . and . . . one . . . opening your eyes now to a new and exciting way of seeing a whole new world . . .'

Anna took a look to either side of her and the people were like her, waking up . . . and smiling about the experience . . . it felt nice, really nice to be that relaxed.

'Welcome back! You guys had some adventure . . .' Troy said energetically.

Everyone was stretching their bodies, yawning and waking from their trance.

'So . . . we were swimming around the coral in the Great Barrier Reef, admiring the wild assortment of tropical fish, and the colours were amazing!' Troy dove straight back into the story that he started earlier in the training.

'Arrrh!' Everyone in the room laughed as they came right back into the room.

'As I was telling you before . . . about my deep-sea diving adventure with my students . . . we were down deep . . . in the awesome blue ocean . . . deep exploring the beauty of the reef and all of the marine life. The colours were spectacular, when all of a sudden we see this three-metre shark silently slicing through the blue water above us. Now, remember I had told my students to always remain calm and be very still, if they were to ever spot a shark like this, on a deep water dive . . . and what do you think they did?' he asked smiling a broad grin across his sun-tanned face.

'They remained calm!' he answered himself in an excited voice jumping off the stage and walking up the centre of the room. 'Every one of my students was, 'at cause' in their life! They'd all conquered their fears. Not only that, but they were in awe of the beauty, the natural beauty right in front of their eyes. And if you think about it—we all have that power in our lives. We all have the power to see the beauty and overcome our fears. Not just today but every day of their lives. So have a think about it—*How can you move forward now with trust in your heart more and more with each new day?*'

When Anna left the building that night, she felt different. She felt in control and excited that this was the beginning of something special.

ႱႱႱႱ

Anna sat comfortably cross-legged on her living room floor taking in the beauty of the panoramic ocean in front of her. She loved the colour contrast of the white sand and the deep blue sea. The large windows framed the view that changed each day depending on the weather. Watching the sky change from clear blue to dark storm clouds and lightening and then back to blue sky again was one of Anna's favourite entertainments. The early morning sun lit up the room as it shone through the double-glazed window. The rolling waves below were hypnotic to Anna as they followed each other, one after the other, caressing the shore. She took a few deep, relaxing breaths and picked up her book *A Course in Miracles,* from the bookshelf and placed it on her lap. The pages fell open:

I loose the world from all I thought it was.

What keeps the world in chains but your beliefs? And what can save the world except your Self? Belief is powerful indeed. The thoughts you hold are mighty, and illusions are as strong in their effects as is the truth.

Anna closed her eyes and drifted quietly into herself. She smiled at the peace and grace she felt now whenever she stopped to be silent.

After her meditation she took the dog's lead from the hook on the back door, whistled, and her Staffordshire bull terrier, Bella came running. Bella loved to swim and run along the beach. The route they took was a four-kilometre tour along the main beach. Depending on the weather and the tides, each day presented a different canvas to explore—the white sand scattered with seashells, seaweed and random driftwood. The beach walk was often interrupted with a coffee and a chat with a friend at the tiny cluster of local shops that included a cafe and newsagent and bookstore.

On the way back to the house she took the narrow pathway through the bush and then she jogged along the back beach to the gate, then up the stairs and onto the balcony of her marvellous home. Anna moved into the kitchen and poured herself a glass of water. Her favourite song came over the radio. She turned the sound up and INXS's, *'What you need,'* played loudly on the stereo. Anna moved her body to the drumbeat. She danced across the wooden floorboards with ease and energy. Michael Hutchison's sexy voice echoed through the kitchen.

Ain't no sense in all your crying
Just pick it up and throw it into shape
Hey you, won't you listen
This is not the end of it all
Don't you see there is a rhythm
I'll take you where you really need to be, whoh-oh

The saxophone was her favourite instrument and it rang through her body. She shimmied across the wooden floorboards that were shiny and clean. Anna danced across the room with joy exuding from her body.

What you need
What you need
I'll give it all, I'll give it all
I'll take you, I'll take you
Where you want to be
That's right

She put her empty glass on the granite bench top near the double sink and she noticed her mobile flashing.

'Hello,' she shouted happily over the music. 'I'm dancing!' She laughed into the phone. 'Come on over!' she said happily, hanging up and dancing past the bench top and leaving the music on full volume.

Grabbing a banana from the fruit bowl she sang into it as if it were her microphone. 'Don't you see there's a rhythm!' she sang out loud as moments later the back door opened and her mother entered carrying a basket full of mangos and avocados.

Merrin laughed at her daughter dancing in the kitchen with a banana for a microphone.

'You're a nut!' she said loudly as Anna turned the music down to a more sensible level for conversation.

'I'm happy, really happy mum.' Anna said giving her mother a big hug.

'I'm happy that you're happy, darling.' Merrin said genuinely, embracing Anna and holding her tightly for a moment. She placed the fruit that she'd brought into the ceramic bowl on the bench.

Bella, Anna's beautiful dog entered through her doggy door and she flopped down in between Anna and Merrin's feet, on the brightly coloured woollen rug.

'I love you girl.' Anna said patting Bella. The dog looked back at her, panting a wide-open, happy smile and wagging her tail in appreciation.

'When does Ryan come home?'

'Tomorrow.'

'Your house looks stunning!'

'You taught me well.'

'To clean?'

'No, *not to clean*! You taught me lots of things, you taught me how to focus on beauty. You taught me how to get through the hard stuff. I didn't appreciate it when I was younger but now I realise that you taught me how to be courageous.'

'Really?'

'Yes really!'

'I'm so grateful for everything, I just want to say thankyou, thankyou, thankyou!'

'You deserve to be happy.'

'I'm happy with everything and I'm at peace with the past—I love you!' Anna said appreciating her mother fully in that moment.

The phone rang interrupting them and Anna jumped up, turned the music down further and answered it.

'Hello.'

'Are you ready for tomorrow?' The deep, resonant male voice on the other end of the phone asked.

Anna played with her blue glass chime in her kitchen as it twinkled in the sunlight and splashed coloured light over the yellow walls.

'Yes. You're coming home tomorrow!'

'And?'

'Ryan, what else is happening tomorrow?' she asked, happily plonking herself down again, on the soft leather lounge next to her mother. Anna was excited that he'd called.

'I'm taking you flying.' Ryan said.

'Yes! It's going to be so much fun. I'm ready for that.'

Anna always had fun whenever Ryan was around. She loved kayaking, that's how they'd met. She'd designed her life so that she could kayak a couple of times a week and living close to the river was essential. To make life easier, she'd altered an old golfing trolley so that her kayak could be strapped to it and steered easily. All she had to do was to pull the trolley the short distance down her street, to the water's edge. The paddling varied, but most often, it started on the left bank near her home and followed the river inland a few kilometres or whenever Anna's biceps began to burn. That was when she knew that it was time to turn back.

One beautiful autumn afternoon Anna pushed off in her kayak heading east up the river and paddled strong. Her paddle broke the water softly, first on her left, and then her right pulling her forward in a smooth gliding motion. The water was cool and clean. Now and then she saw schools of fish darting beneath her. A boat revved its engine loudly on an exit ramp nearby and a red rodeo truck pulled the boat onto its six-wheeler trailer. Two black swans bobbed along elegantly with the shifting ebb of the tide. A small sailboat zigzagged across the wind on the opposite side of the river and a motorboat left a churning white trail of froth behind in its wake for twenty metres. The sound of its engines floated on the wind past Anna, to the pine trees, over the bicycle path and beyond the edges of the waterway. It wasn't busy. Occasionally, a boat or ferry passed. Anna stayed close to the shore to keep clear of any bigger vessels.

The glare of the setting sun was intense when she turned around to come back. The tide was with her now and she paddled to the shallow water to find the shade of a few trees. In the shaded areas the water looked black. She was resting, taking in the scenery when a sleek, grey curved creature rose up through the surface of the water beside her. It startled her at first and then she was ecstatic. As she looked up to tell someone she noticed a man on a kayak heading towards her.

'Did you see that,' he called out to her excitedly, paddling his kayak closer.

'Yes! Dolphins, they're wonderful.'

'They? I only saw one.'

'There's a mother and a baby.' Anna said, pointing to the baby dolphin in the water beneath her.

They were both laughing with delight when Anna looked closely at the stranger for the first time. The sun was setting behind him and the sky was pink and yellow. His wavy, dark brown hair fell slightly over his face and his olive skin shone in the waning sunlight. He had a dimple on one side of his smile and a twinkle in his eyes.

'Do you mind if I paddle with you for a while?' he asked watching the dolphins curve gently through the surface and dive again.

'Wow!' he said noticing the baby and two more dolphins. Then suddenly there was more!

'What's going on?'

'Wow!'

'There's more!'

Dolphins surrounded the two of them, splashing the kayaks, splashing each other and pushing their curving shapes up closer, ducking under the kayaks and coming up again.

'What's happening?'

'They're saying hello, that's for sure.'

'Oh!' Anna's kayak tipped to the side unstable for a moment.

'Come closer to my kayak so they don't tip us!'

Anna paddled closer to him and he reached over and pulled Anna's kayak together with his.

'Ah! Thanks,'

'They're not shy in coming forward . . . I'm Ryan.'
'Hi, I'm Anna.'

Next minute there were dozens of dolphin, the whole surface around them was splashing, dolphins bumped into her kayak and Anna laughed with delight and looked over to Ryan in disbelief.

'Maybe there's fish for them to feed on.'
'They seem to be playing not feeding.'
'Yes they do!'

Ten metres up ahead of them a dolphin leaped high into the air and then headed out towards the ocean. It seemed to signal the other dolphin to follow the leader and one by one and some in pairs, they moved off in that direction.

Ryan paddled on after them a little and turned back to Anna.

'Do you want to follow them for a while?'
'Yes, I'm going that way.' Anna said, paddling up beside Ryan.
'That was the most amazing experience!' Ryan said smiling broadly at Anna.
'I have never seen so many together.'
'It was electrifying!'

The dolphins surfaced now and then on their way out to sea, each time a fin broke the water Anna felt her excitement return. The sun was set when she pulled her kayak onto shore and lifted it on to the trolley. Only the pink sky remained. She was undoing her safety vest when Ryan walked over to her.

'Let's go out to dinner and celebrate our first kayak together!'
'I'd like that.'

ھ ھ ھ ھ

Dinner and conversation with Ryan was surprising and entertaining. Anna wanted to know more about him. He felt somehow familiar to her and she was comfortable giving him a hug good night. When she stood back and looked at Ryan she saw a happy twinkle in his eyes that was appealing. He reached over and gently pulled her back into his arms and they kissed.

ঌ ঌ ঌ ঌ

That night Anna had a dream. In the dream she was Hiawatha's sister. She was running, she had a message, an important message about keeping children safe, not just the children of today; or the children of tomorrow, not just the next generation but all future generations. She had to pass this message on.

Her long brown braids bobbed up and down as she ran; Her body was alive with purpose and resolve. Her intention pushed her forward through the forest; she ran up a steep hill and then scampered down into a gully. Sweat beaded on her forehead and soaked into her soft deerskin dress. One minute she was aware of the small blue and white beads sewn into the fabric and how heavy they felt and the next moment she heard a growling sound and suddenly she stopped still. A massive brown grizzly bear was chasing after her. Anna tried to hide behind a tree but it took a swipe at her and tore a deep wound in her right shoulder.

Then in the dream, somehow Anna was in a tipi and Ryan was helping her. He looked so different. There was a crackling warm fire. He was chanting over her, shaking a wampum belt over her right arm and shoulder. He placed a poultice on her broken skin and pulled the pain out. Anna could feel the pain go. She focussed her attention on his beautiful sounds. His healing touch taught her how to focus on pleasure instead of pain . . . Ryan placed a bear claw on a piece of leather around her neck and wrapped a bear skin around her shoulders.

Anna didn't know what was happening: She didn't know who Hiawatha was. She had never heard of a wampum belt. She didn't know why Ryan was chanting over her, or why he wore eagle feathers in his long dark hair. She certainly didn't know why the spirit of the brown grizzly bear entered through the opening in the tipi and was walking straight to her. At first she was terrified but then she realised that the spirit bear meant her no harm. Ryan didn't seem to notice the bear. He just kept on chanting. The bear sat down next to Anna.

'Do you know yourself now?' the bear asked.

'Yes I do.' Anna said, wondering when this dream was going to end.

'Do you know your mind and your heart?'

'I think I do. I know my strengths and weaknesses.' Anna told the bear.

'To achieve happiness you must know yourself, your light and your darkness.' The bear said, happily nodding his head.

'It feels good.' Anna said resting her hands on her heart.

'Only now can you dream your dreams and own them.' The bear said looking directly into Anna's eyes. His bulky brown body ambled slowly in a circle around Anna's body and then he lay down and rested his big soft brown head at her feet.

The dream was a sign for Anna. She felt good about getting to know Ryan more, and over the winter months they spent a lot of time together. Anna allowed her soft vulnerable heart to open and she let Ryan's goodness in. In fact, those winter months were some of the happiest Anna had ever experienced.

෴෴෴෴

'Mum, Ryan and I are going flying tomorrow and he's giving me a lesson.' Anna said to her mother who was patting Bella in the living room.

'You can have that. I would be too frightened to fly.'

'Oh no its exciting! I have always wanted to learn to fly ever since I was little.'

෴෴෴෴

The next morning was the first day of spring. Anna smiled up at the soft blue sky above and looked along the runway that stretched out in front of her as far as she could see. Her new high-heeled boots made a clicking sound that sounded important, as she walked out onto the tarmac.

'Are you ready to fly?' Ryan, her partner and flight instructor asked. He embraced her in a big bear hug. Anna slipped her arms under his soft leather pilot jacket and hugged his strong body. The warmth of his embrace flowed over her and filled her heart.

'Yes but I'm a bit nervous, how do I know I can trust you?'
'You have a good feeling about me don't you?'
'Yes, but what if I can't.'
'What if you can't trust me?'
'Yes, Trust you, trust us—the whole thing.'
'You know what trust is not, right?'
'Yes I know exactly what that feels like.'
'When trust has been taken away and you realise you don't have it. You have to set the intention to build it. We both need to be willing and open to experience something new. We will build it together; we both earn it with each other. You will feel, and I will feel and we'll talk a lot about how we both feel. We will explore and build trust in each other and it will be wonderful fun. One day at a time.'

'Sounds good to me.'

Ryan was a gentleman and opened the pilot's door and Anna climbed up into the cabin.

'Let's get started.'

'I am so excited!' Anna said. She noticed the smile spread further across her face as she seated herself comfortably in the cockpit of the airplane. She felt adrenaline surge as the engine of the Meridian plane started. The propeller started to spin slowly and then it quickly spun so fast that it became invisible. Anna could hear the low noise and soft vibration of the Meridian's turbo-prop engine and she felt the comfort of the pressurized, air-conditioned cabin. The plane began to move forward along the air-strip.

She held the control lever in her hands and Ryan went over the take off procedures. The plane lurched forward with increasing speed and the wheels left the tarmac as the plane took flight.

White clouds stretched like pillows on either side of the plane and Anna knew that flying was a dream, a dream come true. As she piloted the plane, she realised that she had been a detective, looking into her life following the clues of her beliefs and decisions back to her beginning. She had been a skydiver, willing to fall off into the abyss of what she had known to be true, and allowed herself to fall into something new and now she was the pilot of her life—the pilot of her future.

About Jennipher McDonald BA(Hons)

Jennipher is a Clinical Hypnotherapist, NLP Trainer, writer and playwright who is fascinated with the creative mind and healing. She is trained in Breath work and has been a Natural Therapist for over twenty-five years. She is a mother of three children.

Printed in Australia
AUOC02n0858230614
261769AU00002B/2/P

9 781452 511276